Salute to America
Celebrity
Cookbook

Published by

J.C. PENNEY COMPANY, INC.

IN APPRECIATION ★ ★ ★ ★

The organizations listed below, which are favorites of our celebrity contributors, will benefit from the publication of this Cookbook.

Action for Boston Community Development
Aim for the Handicapped
All-American Collegiate Golf Foundation
American Cancer Society
American Diabetes Association
American Red Cross
Amnesty International
Arizona Kidney Foundation
The Asthmatic Children's Foundation
Basketball Hall of Fame
Carnegie Hall
Carolina Friends School
CHILDHELP U.S.A.
Children of the Night
The Children's Center –
  New Milford, Connecticut
Christian Children's Fund
Citymeals-on-Wheels
Cystic Fibrosis Foundation
Educational Television Endowment
  for South Carolina
Fresh Air Fund
The Gathering Place Fellowship
Girls Clubs of America
The Great Peace March
The Henry I. Brubeck Memorial Scholarship
Institute for Theatre Training

International Fund for Animal Welfare
John Wayne Cancer Center
Just One Break
Kansas Committee for Prevention
  of Child Abuse
March of Dimes
Marlboro College
Muscular Dystrophy Association
Myasthenia Gravis Foundation
National Audubon Society
National Foundation for Facial Reconstruction
New York City Mission Society
New York Hospital Perinatalogy Center
Nightingale Bamford School
Radcliffe College – Schlesinger Library
  on History of Women in America
St. Charles Church – North Hollywood
St. Michael's Special School – New Orleans
St. Vincent's Hospital – PRIDE Institute
The Salvation Army
Save the Children
Southern Seminary Junior College
Teresa Laxalt Memorial Scholarship Fund
Trans Africa
UNICEF
University of Miami
University of Minnesota –
  The Minnesota Campaign
WETA
Wildlife Conservation International

SALUTE TO AMERICA CELEBRITY COOKBOOK
Copyright 1986 by J.C. Penney Company, Inc.
All rights reserved.

Library of Congress Catalog Card Number: 86-61382
ISBN 0-9611906-2-0
Salute to America Celebrity Cookbook

Concept: Harvey C. McCormick ★ Editors: Peggy Healy Parker and Iris Ihde Frey ★ Production Coordinator: Nancee Dixon
Design: Heydt Graphic Design ★ Food Photographer: Will Rousseau ★ Printer: Lebanon Valley Offset

TABLE OF CONTENTS ★ ★ ★ ★

FOREWORD ★★★★★

To celebrate the 100th birthday of the Statue of Liberty, JCPenney asked a diverse group of American celebrities to contribute a favorite recipe to a *Salute to America Celebrity Cookbook*. The result is a star-studded covered dish supper—a grand celebration of good American cooking.

Each of the 50 states and the District of Columbia is represented by a celebrity cook. Most of the celebrities are native born to the state they represent; others have adopted a state through long-time residence, college education or, simply, affection. Who better than Bob Hope, Good Humor Ambassador at Large, could represent the nation's capital.

Silhouetted behind the text on each page is the year of the state's admittance to the Union. Interspersed throughout the book are special sections devoted to regional American produce. These sections are hosted by some of the country's leading food authorities.

Many of the recipes reflect true culinary pride of place. Cybill Shepherd sent her formula for especially airy Southern Spoon Bread. From Peter Graves—a Minnesotan Wild Rice Casserole. From the bounty of his New England garden, Dave Brubeck created a creamy pumpkin soup. Senator Hollings' antique "receipt" is for an old Charleston oddity, Egg Balls. Pearl Bailey, who grew up along the Virginia shore, fondly recalls hard-shell crab feasts. One cook related so strongly to place that from her home in the Sawatch Mountains of Utah, Mrs. Fields concocted a high-in-calories high-riser she named Chocolate Mountain Peaks.

From New England Clam Chowder to Alaskan Crab Puffs, most of the recipes in this book are indigenously American. Just as American is that many recipes come right out of the melting pot. Ann Landers' recipe for Sweet and Sour Cabbage Soup, Senator Laxalt's Basque Lenten Pie, and Nancy Lopez's Enchilada Casserole reflect old world roots. Typical of the eclectic nature of American style in food is the recipe provided by the Jewish mayor of New York City—Pasta Primavera, an Italian dish with oriental overtones.

Unmistakable trends are evident, too. The popularity of seafood dishes is shown by the fact that nearly a dozen arrived. That half of these are crab recipes—soft-shell, hard-shell, crab in puffs and in gumbo and in beer and in cakes—suggests that perhaps crab is America's most highly favored 1980s food. Tex-Mex proves to be a big favorite, too. And there is an avalanche of dessert recipes—and especially those made with chocolate. On page 66, a sampling of favorites is turned into a delicious chocolate fantasy.

To list all the ingredients of these assembled recipes would be a tribute to the great natural abundance of America. To list the celebrities who participated with generosity and enthusiasm, despite the great demands on their time, is to marvel at the abundance of talent at work in this country. And so we invite you to dine with the celebrities and enjoy the dishes that have nurtured, inspired, or simply pleased them, and as you do, we hope you will reflect on the blessings that Americans share.

ANTIPASTO SALAD

1 head iceberg lettuce, very cold and dry

Ripe olives, chilled and drained

Pimento, drained and slivered

Garbanzo beans, chilled and drained

Genovese salami, cut in slivers

Mozzarella cheese, diced

Romano cheese, grated

Marinated artichoke hearts,
   chilled and drained

Mild pickled Italian peppers (pepperoncini),
   drained

Celery hearts and tops, chopped very fine

Arrange bed of lettuce greens in large, chilled, glass salad bowl. Tear remainder of head of lettuce into bite size pieces and place in bowl. Top with olives, pimento, garbanzo beans, salami, mozzarella and romano cheese, artichoke hearts, peppers, and celery. Bring to table untossed to show off colorful arrangement.

Dressing

Vinegar (a good wine vinegar)

Oil (Sasso or Bertoli)

Salt

Freshly ground black pepper

To serve, add salt, pepper, and vinegar and toss lightly. (Use approximately 3 parts oil to 1 part vinegar.) Add oil and toss again.

BOB AND DOLORES HOPE

At his 80th birthday bash, lavishly celebrated at Kennedy Center, Dolores Hope wowed a national television audience with a sweetly sung solo to her husband of 50 years. They had met in 1933, during the run of the musical *Roberta.* Now 83, he continues to entertain and amaze a world full of fans. He has been awarded the President's Medal of Freedom and the Kennedy Center Honor for Lifetime Achievement in The Arts—and a thousand additional awards and citations for humanitarian and professional efforts. One of seven sons, he made his vaudeville debut in Cleveland, then soft-shoed his way onto the Broadway stage, and on to radio, motion pictures, and television. During World War II, he began his tours to entertain United States troops stationed around the globe. It is to the Hopes that their admirers say, "Thanks for the memories."

"This can be served as a first course salad or even as a main dish. Serve with hot crusty bread."

Perfect Starters

Before dinner, after the ballet, even on a Friday evening
after a long, hard week, a sparkling wine from New York State or
California turns the occasion into a celebration.
Perfect accompaniments are hot Alaskan crab puffs à la
Governor William Jennings Sheffield, icy cold Florida stone crab claws,
and distinctively different macadamia nuts from Hawaii.

6

HARPER LEE

One critic said of this southern author that she "seemed to be born with compassion." Within a year of publication, her first novel won a Pulitzer Prize and the hearts of American booklovers. The writer of *To Kill a Mockingbird* was born in Monroeville, Alabama, and has lived there "obscurely and happily" for many years. Her early study of law brought to life the novel's courageous attorney, Atticus Finch, later portrayed on film by Gregory Peck. The book continues to inspire new generations of readers. (The hardback is in its 44th printing.) Although traveling a great deal, she finds time for her chief interests other than writing: collecting memoirs of nineteenth century clergymen, golf, criminology, and music.

SPRING SOUP

Maybe this could be called Writer's Soup. I live alone and am a one-pot cook. I cook by ear. This soup starts with ham hocks. *Smoked* ham hocks. Now there are hocks and hocks. Look for the best you can find. Bigger ones are preferable. Take the rind off the hocks—about three or four. Put them in a medium size kettle, not a cauldron, with water to cover. Put in a pinch of sweet basil, fresh if you have it and a tiny bit of chili powder. You won't taste the chili powder. I throw in a garlic clove. Don't chop it up—before serving you can yank the clove out and nobody will know it's been there. Bring to a boil and cook for 35 to 45 minutes until the meat is tender. Just before taking it off the stove, it's time to add the vegetables. Use whatever is fresh. De-cob an ear of corn. Chop up some fresh summer squash or zucchini and by all means some fresh peas. If you want potatoes, cut them in, peeled or unpeeled. Except if they're red potatoes, peel them so the soup won't discolor. Sure, throw in some parsnips and carrots. Turnips, too. Little white turnips, not a big yellow one—a starving writer couldn't afford that. If you use a tomato, peel it by all means and seed it and don't use much, only about as much as a palmful. You could put in a slice or two of cabbage, not a lot. And by all means, this is very important, green pepper. Chop it up and throw in a handful just before serving so it stays crisp. Add some black pepper, too, but you probably won't want any salt as the smoked hocks provide enough. Makes enough for a good chapter's worth.

1819

ALASKA ★★★★★★★

CRABMEAT PUFFS

2 egg whites

1 cup small pieces crab

1 cup mayonnaise

Salt and pepper, to taste

Toasted bread rounds
 (about 3½ dozen, 1½")

Paprika

Beat egg whites until stiff. Fold in crab and mayonnaise. Season to taste with salt and pepper. Spread mixture on toasted bread rounds. Sprinkle with paprika. Broil for 2 minutes or until puffy and lightly browned. Serve immediately. Makes 3½ dozen.

GOVERNOR WILLIAM JENNINGS SHEFFIELD

Born in the state of Washington, he heeded Horace Greeley's admonition, "Go west, young man!" and rose from salesman to governor of the 49th state.

"At the Governor's House, we try to serve as much Alaskan food — fish, game, meats, and produce — as possible. Crabmeat puffs serve as the delicious first course of a favorite menu. The rest of the meal includes Parmesan halibut, wild rice pilaf, steamed broccoli — and for dessert we serve Alaskan low bush cranberry and apple pie."

1959

LAYERED RANCHERO DIP

2 10½ ounce cans jalapeno bean dip

1 cup sour cream

⅔ cup mayonnaise

1 1¼ ounce package taco seasoning mix

2 4 ounce cans chopped green chilies, drained

4 medium size avocados

2 teaspoons lime juice

1 teaspoon salt

¼ teaspoon garlic powder

8 ounces (2 cups) shredded sharp
   cheddar cheese

2 cups chopped green onions

2 cups chopped tomatoes

6 ounces ripe olives, sliced

Tortilla chips

Thinly spread bean dip into shallow 15″ × 10″
dish. Combine sour cream, mayonnaise, and
taco seasoning mix and spread over bean dip.
Over this spread 1 can chilies. Peel, pit, and
mash avocados; combine with lime juice, salt,
and garlic powder. Layer over chilies. Spread
with remaining chilies. Sprinkle with alternate
layers of cheese, onions, and tomatoes. Top
with ripe olives. Serve with tortilla chips.
Makes 11 cups.

ERMA BOMBECK

From the Arizona desert, she dryly delights
30 million readers around the world and keeps
coming up with bestsellers like *The Grass Is
Always Greener Over the Septic Tank, If Life Is a
Bowl of Cherries, What Am I Doing in the Pits?,*
and *I Lost Everything in the Post Natal Depression.*

"This is an old family recipe that has been
in the family for about 15 minutes. It takes for-
ever to make and looks like an eye infection,
BUT it tastes wonderful. I bring it out when-
ever I have a meal that is forgettable."

1912

"DELIGHT"FUL SOUTHERN FRIED CHICKEN

Chicken pieces
  (whatever pieces your family prefers)
Shortening
Flour
Salt and pepper

Heat several tablespoons of shortening in your favorite skillet. We use an old cast iron one. Rinse chicken pieces. Season flour with salt and pepper and dust chicken pieces with it. Fry chicken, turning until all sides are golden brown and crunchy. When chicken is done, add several tablespoons water to the pan, cover and simmer until gravy forms and thickens.

GLEN CAMPBELL

Born in the Wonder State, the seventh son of a seventh son, he says his good luck surfaced with his phenomenally popular recording of *Gentle on My Mind.* He has collected a string of awards including Grammys and two for Best Entertainer of the Year, but he calls himself "Joe American—the apple pie kinda guy." He dubs his dish after his birthplace, Delight, Arkansas.

"'Delight'ful Southern Fried Chicken is crunchy, messy, and better than finger lickin' good! Enjoy!"

SPAGHETTI VONGOLE
(Spaghetti with Clam Sauce)

½ cup scallions, finely chopped

2 tablespoons garlic, finely chopped

¾ cup celery, finely chopped

2 tablespoons cooking or olive oil

2 10½ ounce cans white clam sauce

⅓ cup chablis wine

Freshly ground pepper, to taste

1 pound angel hair spaghetti (copa di angeli)

Sauté scallions, garlic, and celery slowly in oil in frying pan (approximately 5 minutes). Add clam sauce, wine, and pepper and allow to cook another 3 minutes. Serve over spaghetti. Serves 6.

CLIFF ROBERTSON

Born in La Jolla and bombed in Pearl Harbor when he was a teenage gob, he took to acting like a duck to water. He rose from playing bit parts with a troupe in the Catskills, to starring on Broadway in *Orpheus Descending,* to winning an Emmy for *The Game* and an Oscar for his touching portrayal of the title role in the film *Charly.* A flying buff who collects vintage biplanes, he wings his way across the airwaves as television spokesman for AT&T.

"This dish, which tastes of the sea, is popular in my hometown, La Jolla, a resort known for its beaches and foam-washed caves."

1850

The West

In the 1960s, two phenomena occurred that were to put California on the international culinary map: the use of the mesquite grill at the restaurant *Chez Panisse* in San Francisco and the technological break-through of the cold fermentation process for wines used so successfully by Robert Mondavi at Oakville in the Napa Valley.

The former event was the beginning of a cooking revolution in the West that was to result in a nouvelle American cuisine; the latter of a revolution in viniculture that created the means of producing serious American wines.

While west coast chefs have been mapping out new culinary territory with pomegranates, kiwis, avocados, artichokes, apricots, and almonds, the vintners have been busy developing wines to compete in world markets. Today, the California valleys with their sonorous names — Napa, Sonoma, Salinas, San Joaquin — contain more than 500,000 acres yielding in excess of 300,000 barrels of wine from vineyards in such romantic sounding places as Calistoga, Rutherford, El Dorado, Temecula, Soledad, Sebastopol, San Luis Obispo, Calaveras, and San Jose.

ALICE WATERS

Through her restaurant, *Chez Panisse,* in Berkeley, California, she is credited with revolutionizing American cooking in the 1970s. Her menus draw from French culinary tradition adapted to the freshest and finest of California produce and wines. And to this she adds an innovative, creative touch. Her restaurant has rarely repeated a menu exactly since it opened in 1971. She credits, with undue modesty, her restaurant's success to the atmosphere of support and freedom that abounds in the Berkeley area. Her books include *The Chez Panisse Menu Cookbook* and *Chez Panisse Pasta, Pizza and Calzone,* both published by Random House.

"In search of delicious fresh ingredients and a healthful way of eating, Californians have gone back to the garden and are rediscovering fruits and vegetables that have a wonderful variety of flavors and textures. All the different kinds of young lettuces, wild mushrooms, vine ripened tomatoes, edible flowers, heirloom varieties of fruits, each in its season, are our pride and joy...and inspiration... in the kitchen."

13

TRINCHERA TACOS

Taco Sauce

¼ cup diced onion

1 large garlic clove, finely chopped

1 tablespoon vegetable oil

8 ounces canned tomatoes, drained and coarsely chopped

8 ounces tomato sauce

¼ teaspoon sugar

½ teaspoon salt, or to taste

¼ teaspoon black pepper

½ teaspoon chili pequin or other hot red pepper (optional)

MALCOLM FORBES

He has raised ballooning to new heights, carried motorcycling to the Great Wall of China, and launched yacht design into the 21st century with his fabulous Highlander V. In addition to running his publishing empire, he still finds time to retreat to his ranch in the Rocky Mountain State.

"While tacos vary as widely as pizza in texture, hotness, and ingredients, this recipe is a way ahead winner with the Forbes family."

Sauté onions and garlic in oil. Add tomatoes, tomato sauce, sugar, salt and pepper. Simmer 5 minutes. Add chili pequin, if desired.

1¼ pounds ground sirloin

2 garlic cloves (whole)

¼ teaspoon black pepper

¾ teaspoon salt

12 corn tortillas (available in refrigerator case of grocery store)

1 cup vegetable oil

½ pound Longhorn cheese, grated

1 small head lettuce, shredded

Sauté ground sirloin slightly. Add garlic cloves, pepper and salt. Sauté until brown. Remove garlic cloves. Immerse tortillas in 375° oil. Spread tortillas over paper towels until slightly cooled. Sprinkle grated cheese in center of tortilla (reserve some cheese for garnish), top with beef mixture and fold in half. Crisp on hot grill. Fill taco with shredded lettuce. Top with taco sauce and garnish with remaining grated cheese. Serves 4.

1876

MOLTING CRUSTACEANS

4 to 6 soft shell crabs*
Cayenne pepper
2 tablespoons vegetable oil
1 tablespoon sesame oil
½ cup finely minced onion
1 tablespoon grated fresh ginger
3 limes (juice 2 limes, cut 3rd for garnish)
2 tablespoons low-sodium soy sauce
¾ cup snipped cilantro (coriander)

Have ready a heavy cast iron skillet with cover. Place pinch of cayenne pepper under both flaps of crab, making sure all traces of fibrous tissue have been removed. Heat oils until they begin to ripple like water; but do not allow to smoke. Add onions, grated ginger, stir, then add crabs. (They spatter a great deal so be prepared, if necessary, to cover loosely with lid.) Cook approximately 1 minute over medium heat until golden orange in color. Turn so that both sides cook thoroughly. Add lime juice, soy sauce, and cilantro. Stir to glaze and coat crabs. Transfer to platter and garnish with lime wedges. Serves 2.

*Ask fish monger to clean crabs of gills and face.

LEONARD BERNSTEIN

Laureate Conductor of the New York Philharmonic, he was the orchestra's first leader to be American born and trained. His compositions are played in movie houses, Broadway theatres, and cathedrals. A dyed-in-the-wool New Englander — Harvard graduate, long associated with the Berkshire Music Center — he has been a long-time resident of the Nutmeg State.

"Molting crustaceans are one of the glories of spring. This Asian-inspired soft shell crab recipe is deliciously prepared in my kitchen by chef Patti Pulliam."

DELAWARE ★★★★★★

STRAWBERRIES AND CUSTARD SAUCE

2 quarts strawberries

2 cups heavy cream (divided)

2 tablespoons sugar

4 egg whites

1 teaspoon vanilla

2 cups strawberry jam

¼ cup kirsch

Rinse and hull berries and drain. Put in bowl and chill. Scald 1 cup cream in top of double boiler. Stir in sugar. Remove pan from hot water. In small mixing bowl, beat egg whites with remaining cream. Warm mixture with a little scalded cream. Stir well, then gradually add to hot cream. Set pan back over boiling water and cook custard, stirring constantly, until it thickens. (Custard will continue to thicken as it cools.) Stir in vanilla. Pour into glass container, cover tightly, and chill. Before serving, thin strawberry jam with kirsch and spread over well drained strawberries. Serve with custard sauce. Serves 6 to 8.

PIERRE DU PONT IV

Former Governor of Delaware, he is known informally as "Pete." He is a descendant of Eleuthere Irenee du Pont, the French refugee who was encouraged by Thomas Jefferson to set up a factory on the Brandywine River to provide the new nation with gunpowder for hunting, land clearance, mining, and defense. Other benefits attributable to the family are cellophane, nylon, Orlon, Dacron, and the Winterthur Museum, which houses 80,000 American antiques.

"A good meal is not complete without the taste of a marvelous sweet at the end."

1787

APRICOT MOUSSE
WITH GRAND MARNIER

4 egg whites
1 18 ounce jar apricot jam
Grand Marnier liqueur

Preheat oven to 350°. Butter soufflé dish. In a bowl, beat egg whites stiff. Fold in apricot jam. Transfer to soufflé dish and place in pan containing 1″ hot water. Bake 45 minutes. Remove from oven and keep at room temperature until ready to serve. Pass *Grand Marnier* liqueur to be poured over each serving. Serves 6 (or 8 light servings).

DINA MERRILL

Daughter of Marjorie Merriweather Post and Edward F. Hutton, she grew up in the splendid Palm Beach mansion Mar-a-Lago but claims to be from hard-working pioneer stock brought up with the work ethic — and proves it with untiring devotion to many charities.

"I'm not much of a cook but this mousse is so easy to do — and is *so* impressive it wows 'em everytime!"

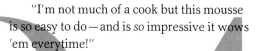

BLACKENED SWORDFISH WITH CHARDONNAY AND LIME BUTTER

8 ounce swordfish fillet, about 1″ thick, per person

Marinade (per fillet)

2 tablespoons olive oil

½ tablespoon wine vinegar

¼ ounce chardonnay wine

¼ teaspoon coarse salt

1 clove garlic, minced

Mix thoroughly.

Blackening Seasoning (per fillet)

¾ teaspoon oregano

¾ teaspoon thyme

¾ teaspoon marjoram

¼ teaspoon cayenne pepper

½ teaspoon black pepper

½ teaspoon salt

Mix thoroughly.

Lime Butter (enough for 8 fillets)

1 cup whipped butter

2 limes (zest and juice)

1 teaspoon sugar

1 teaspoon salt

½ teaspoon pepper

½ ounce chardonnay wine

Blend in food processor. (Refrigerate any remaining lime butter.)

Not everyone marinates fish when they are to be blackened, but I believe that this is the only way for the dish to be prepared. I use my own house dressing and chardonnay wine; however, your own favorite dressing will suit very well also. (Oil and vinegar and garlic or Italian-type, please.) Marinate fish for 1 hour (fish take marinade very quickly). Coat fish with blackening seasoning. Get a large, cast iron skillet very hot and lay the seasoned fish inside. There will be enough oil in the marinade that the fish won't stick. After 5 minutes, check with your finger to see if flesh is firm, and turn fillet over — 1 or 2 minutes more will be enough. Be careful not to overcook. Top with lime butter and a twist of lime as garnish.

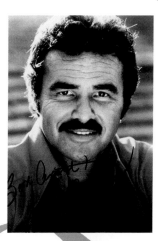

BURT REYNOLDS

Born in Waycross, Georgia, this modern day Rhett Butler bounded from a position with the Baltimore Colts, to *Gunsmoke,* to centerfold pinup, to world's number one box office star. He now supervises the *Burt Reynolds Dinner Theatre,* which he built in Florida. On leave from movie making, he is determined to enjoy "people and life and air and ocean and all that good stuff..."

"Chef Dave Duncan of my *Backstage* restaurant contributed this recipe. I hate fish unless it's cooked this way."

STUFFED ABURAGE*

1 pound boneless uncooked chicken, minced

½ pound uncooked fishcakes, chopped

1 can water chestnuts, drained and
    coarsely chopped

½ bunch scallions, chopped

2 tablespoons dried shrimp, soaked
    and drained (chopped if needed)

2 tablespoons black beans (Tau See),
    soaked and drained

2 tablespoons oyster sauce

2 tablespoons soy sauce (Shoyu)

1 teaspoon garlic powder

8 large aburage

Oil for frying

1 cup water

Combine chicken, fishcakes, water chestnuts, scallions, shrimp, black beans, oyster sauce, soy sauce, and garlic powder. Mix well. Place aburage in boiling water briefly to soften. Cut a slit along the long side of each aburage and stuff with mixture. Fold opening over to close and fry with opening side down in hot oil until brown. Turn, add water, cover and simmer for 1 hour. Add more water if necessary. When done, make gravy as follows:

1 tablespoon cornstarch

½ cup water

1 tablespoon oyster sauce

1 tablespoon soy sauce

Blend ingredients until smooth, then simmer over low heat until transparent and thickened. Serves 4.

*Aburage is Japanese-style bean curd. It comes in flat, fried squares or larger rectangles and is available in the freezer section of Oriental food stores.

DON HO

A bundle of tropical energy, Mr. Waikiki is known for his white suits, hit song *Tiny Bubbles,* and night club line, "Let me have 20 grandmothers up here on stage!" He was also a Massachusetts collegian, an Air Force pilot, and the recipient of the Army's Civilian Service Award.

"This popular regional dish is a favorite of mine. It's delicious any time of day."

1959

SUN VALLEY GAME CHOUCROUTE

8 pounds fresh sauerkraut

5 to 6 ounces goose fat or lard

5 cups finely chopped onions

3 to 4 large garlic cloves

2 large apples, peeled, cored, and chopped

3 cups chopped carrots

2 quarts chicken stock

½ cup gin

1 bottle Reisling or champagne

Bouquet garni

12 juniper berries

2 pounds salt pork or smoked bacon

2 large pheasants or 2 ducks

4 quail

Vegetable oil

Salt and pepper

2 pounds pork shoulder

8 weisswurst

4 bratwurst

4 pounds garlic sausage (cottachino)

Carefully rinse sauerkraut, wringing it out using cold water. Melt goose fat or lard in large stockpot. Add onions and garlic. Simmer until onions wilt. Stir in apples and carrots, then add sauerkraut and toss. Put in stock, gin, and half of wine. Preheat oven to 325? Bring sauerkraut mixture to a boil and stir. Transfer half of sauerkraut mixture to large casserole. Add bouquet garni, juniper berries, salt pork or bacon and cover with remaining sauerkraut. Cover casserole and bake for 2½ hours, turning occasionally. Remove from oven and place sauerkraut mixture back in stockpot. Meanwhile, rub birds with oil, salt, and pepper. Put in roasting pan and roast in 425° oven for 30 minutes. Remove from oven and quarter pheasants (or duck), halve quail, slice pork shoulder. When sauerkraut has cooked 2½ hours, take from stove and put back in stockpot. Then layer casserole with sauerkraut, pheasants (or duck), quail, sliced pork, then sauerkraut, etc. Cook for 1½ hours adding more wine, if needed. Put wursts and garlic sausage in a saucepan of cold water, and simmer for 45 minutes. Arrange choucroute on a platter with sausages and sliced cottachino. Serve with different rye and pumpernickel breads and many mustards. Beer or a nice Reisling goes well with it. Serves 12 or more.

Editor's note: This recipe assumes two ovens. To prepare in one oven, allow extra time to cook birds and pork shoulder. You will have to remove casserole from the oven and raise temperature to 425° to cook birds.

PETER DUCHIN AND BROOKE HAYWARD

Kim Novak and Tyrone Power played his parents in the Hollywood movie, *The Eddie Duchin Story.* Following in his bandleader-father's footsteps, he formed a Dixieland jazz group while a teen-age preppy; later he played at the White House for Luci Johnson's wedding, then around the globe for royalty galore. Today he is, without question, America's society bandleader. He is now married to Brooke Hayward, the beautiful actress and best-selling author of *Haywire,* her story of growing up in a theatrical family.

"My godfather, Averell Harriman," says Peter, "built Sun Valley for the Union Pacific railroad. We have spent countless hours skiing there. This *choucroute* is a wonderful dish for warming the cockles after a day on the slopes."

The Northwest

Every year fishermen of the Northwest net about 600 million pounds of salmon, 800 thousand pounds of sturgeon, and 40 thousand pounds of trout. In fact, the roe from this enormous catch are so plentiful that America can now claim her own burgeoning caviar industry. In the cold, clear waters of Alaska, crab is king, and the salmon run each year as sure as spring returns. Further south, the waters of Washington and Oregon provide geoduck clams, Olympia oysters, razor clams, and Dungeness crabs. Freshwater lakes and streams produce trout and spotted bass.

From Eskimo to Indian, from gold panner to today's urban dweller, all who have been nourished by the land and waters of the Northwest can praise its unique bounty.

JEFF SMITH

This exuberant personality has quickly established himself in the world of celebrity chefs. He conducts a very popular cooking class on public television, and his book *The Frugal Gourmet* has sold almost a million copies. An ordained minister and former college chaplain, he became interested in food after teaching a course called *Food as Sacrament and Celebration.* He lives with his wife and two sons in a house overlooking Puget Sound. "It's hard to point to a single characteristic of Pacific Northwest cuisine and call that characteristic typical. The superb seafood and the local Indians who taught us to cook it, the presence of people from Scandinavia, the Chinese railroad workers who stayed in Seattle, the Korean, Vietnamese, and Thai citizens who have come here with American servicemen —all of these factors and peoples have contributed. The produce is fresh and lush and the wines from Washington state are now world famous. I am a happy child of the Pacific Northwest and its wonderful food convinces me that there's no place like home. Come to the Pike Place Farmers market and you will understand."

OLD BAY CRABCAKES

2 slices bread, crusts removed

¼ cup milk

1 pound crabmeat

1 teaspoon old bay seasoning*

¼ teaspoon salt

1 tablespoon mayonnaise

1 tablespoon Worcestershire sauce

1 tablespoon chopped parsley

1 tablespoon baking powder

1 egg, beaten

2 tablespoons butter

2 tablespoons oil

In a bowl, break bread into small pieces and moisten with milk. Mix together with other ingredients. Shape into cakes. Melt 2 tablespoons butter with 2 tablespoons oil and fry crabcakes until golden brown (about 7 minutes each side). Serves 4.

*or substitute ½ teaspoon dry mustard and ½ teaspoon paprika.

MARIA SHRIVER

Daughter of a Cape Cod Kennedy and a Chesapeake Bay Shriver, she grew up in the Windy City while her father, Sargeant Shriver, tended the huge Merchandise Mart. She has earned her own fame as the "tacked-down," blue-eyed co-anchor of the *CBS Morning Show* and as the bride of Arnold Schwarzenegger.

"My father's family grew up in Maryland—which is famous for its crabcakes."

1818

BILL BLASS

Who would have thought that this former member of the Fort Wayne High School football team, who served as a combat engineer in the Army Engineer Corps in World War II, would gain fame as a premier designer of American fashion? Although he dines at the finest restaurants and attends the most elegant dinner parties, this Hoosier's choice of meat loaf as his favorite recipe reflects his design philosophy — simplicity is always in good taste.

MEAT LOAF

2 tablespoons butter

1 cup chopped celery

1 cup chopped onions

3 pounds chopped sirloin or round

1 teaspoon salt

½ teaspoon pepper

½ cup sour cream

2 eggs beaten with 1 tablespoon Worcestershire sauce

1 cup bread crumbs

½ cup chopped parsley

1 bottle chili sauce

3 strips bacon

Preheat oven to 350°. Melt butter over medium heat in large saucepan and sauté celery and onions until transparent. In large bowl, combine celery, onions, chopped meat, salt, pepper, sour cream, eggs, Worcestershire sauce, bread crumbs, and parsley and form into loaf. Place in roasting pan. Top with chili sauce and bacon strips. Cook 1½ hours. Serves 8.

1816

SWEET AND SOUR CABBAGE SOUP

2 pounds lean soup meat

1 large onion, coarsely chopped

2 cups canned tomatoes

1 head cabbage, shredded

Salt

1 28 ounce can tomato sauce

Juice of 2 lemons, or more, to taste

Up to ¾ cup granulated sugar

Up to 1 cup brown sugar

Salt and pepper, to taste

Sour cream (optional)

Put soup meat in kettle with 3 quarts water and bring to boil. Skim surface. Add onion and tomatoes and bring to boil. (While meat cooks, put cabbage into colander, sprinkle liberally with salt, and set aside.) Simmer meat until very tender, about 2 hours. Remove meat from kettle and cut into bite size cubes. Add tomato sauce and lemon juice. Add granulated sugar and brown sugar according to taste. Adjust for sweet and sour. Drench cabbage with hot water to remove salt. Add to soup and cook for about 10 minutes. Skim fat from surface. Add salt and pepper, to taste. If desired, top each bowl of soup with a dollop of sour cream. Serves 10 generously.

ANN LANDERS

Born Eppie Friedman on the Fourth of July in Sioux City, she has used her compassion, common sense, and wit to become America's favorite confessor. Not just advice to the lovelorn, "Ann Landers" draws from a broad network of professionals in medical, religious, and legal fields to cheer and comfort an admiring public. Polls consistently place her on "most admired" lists.

1846

The Heartland

Hog butcher to the world, bread basket of the nation, where corn is king and dairy is queen, the Midwest personifies amber waves of grain, rolling fields dotted with contented cows, and acre upon unending acre of prairie land. Settled by immigrants seeking freedom from poverty or religious persecution, America's heartland reflects — in its crops and cooking — those early pioneers. Scandinavians gathered in Minnesota and Wisconsin. Germans in large numbers established themselves in Illinois and Missouri. Michigan became home to newcomers from Holland. And very quickly cabbages became sauerkraut, pastry became "Danish," pork was turned into kielbasa, milk became limburger, and corn sometimes became "likker."

ABBY MANDEL

One of the most accomplished teaching chefs and cookbook authors in the nation, this food processor whiz brought "Machine Cuisine" to the home cook through her classes and widely syndicated columns. She has trained with the great chefs of Europe including Jacques Cagna, Frédy Girardet, and Michel Guérard. Her latest book is *Fast and Flavorful*.

"From the rivers, lakes and streams, farms, fields and gently rolling prairies of America's heartland comes food that has nurtured a nation and given it strength, and girth, and greatness. Find here the best that America has to offer — real food that is simple and honest and close to our heart and soul."

KANSAS KIEV

½ cup butter

2 cloves garlic, crushed

½ teaspoon salt

⅛ teaspoon pepper

2 teaspoons snipped chives

2 tablespoons snipped fresh parsley

½ teaspoon crumbled dry rosemary

4 large chicken breasts, halved,
  skinned, and boned

Salt and pepper

Flour, for coating

Beaten egg

Unseasoned bread crumbs

3 tablespoons vegetable oil

3 tablespoons butter

In small bowl, combine butter, garlic, salt, pepper, chives, parsley, and rosemary and blend well. Lay on sheet of waxed paper. Fold paper over butter mixture, then pat into ¾" thick rectangle. Wrap well and freeze until very hard. Meanwhile, to flatten and enlarge, pound chicken breast between 2 sheets waxed paper, boned side up. (Use mallet or rolling pin.) Cut frozen butter mixture into 8 sticks. Place one on each breast half. Salt and pepper, to taste. Fold short sides up, then roll breast around butter stick using it as axis. Press edges firmly together to seal butter stick in tightly. Dredge each in flour, dip in egg, then roll in bread crumbs until completely coated. Place seam side down in large skillet in bubbly mixture of oil and butter. Brown quickly on all surfaces, using 2 forks to turn. Lower heat and sauté 12 to 15 minutes or until done. Serves 8. Note: Chicken may be prepared ahead and refrigerated after the breading process is completed.

SENATOR ROBERT DOLE

He was born in the town of Russell, Kansas, the son of a grain elevator manager. He earned the Bronze Star, the Purple Heart, and the rank of Captain as a combat platoon leader in World War II before winning the hand of Elizabeth Hanford. Together, the Sunflower State senator and his wife, the Secretary of Transportation, make up one of Washington's favorite couples.

1861

HOT CHICKEN SALAD

4 cups cooked chicken

2 cans condensed cream of chicken soup

2 cups chopped celery

1 cup slivered almonds

1 cup mayonnaise

2 cans water chestnuts, drained

1½ cups grated cheddar cheese

Salt and pepper, to taste

1 cup crushed potato chips

Preheat oven to 350° Chop chicken into bite size pieces. Combine with chicken soup, celery, almonds, mayonnaise, water chestnuts, and cheddar cheese. Salt and pepper, to taste. Transfer to large casserole. Sprinkle crushed potato chips over top. Bake 45 minutes or until hot and bubbly. Serves 10 to 12.

PHYLLIS GEORGE

Following her selection as Miss America in 1971, she was launched into a career as hostess *extraordinaire.* She has hosted seven Miss America pageants, eight Rose Bowl parades, five Super Bowl broadcasts and numerous television shows including *Candid Camera, NFL Today,* and the *CBS Morning News.* When her husband, John Brown, Jr., was Governor of Kentucky, she served as the gracious hostess of the Governor's Mansion.

"This is a dish I frequently serve when I host luncheons at our 164 year old Kentucky farmhouse, Cave Hill Place. Guests seem to thoroughly enjoy this dish and are always asking for the recipe."

1792

CHICKEN CHARTRES©

Seasoning Mix

2 tablespoons salt

1½ teaspoons onion powder

1½ teaspoons garlic powder

1½ teaspoons black pepper

1 teaspoon white pepper

1 teaspoon ground cumin

½ teaspoon red cayenne pepper

½ teaspoon sweet paprika

Combine the seasoning mix ingredients in a small bowl; mix thoroughly and set aside.

3 (3 to 3½ pound) chickens

1½ cups finely chopped onions

½ cup (1 stick) plus 6 tablespoons unsalted butter

Vegetable oil for deep frying

3 pounds russet potatoes, peeled and cut into ½ inch slices

3 ounces sliced bacon, finely chopped (about ½ cup)

4 ounces ham, chopped (about ¾ cup)

1 cup Basic Chicken Stock (recipe follows)

1 recipe Cajun Béarnaise Sauce (recipe follows)

6 eggs

Cut leg-thigh pieces from chickens and debone along length of bones, leaving meat in one piece with skin on. Debone breasts lengthwise to get two breast pieces per chicken, also with skin on.

To prepare each "half-chicken" serving, use one breast and one leg piece. In roasting pan, lay each leg, skin-side-up, on top of a breast, skin-side-up; tuck edges of leg meat and skin under breast piece to form what will appear to be one piece of chicken. Generously season chicken "halves" on both sides with a total of 2 tablespoons plus ½ teaspoon Season-ing Mix, patting it in by hand. Plump up each piece so it is neatly formed and rounded with skin side up. Sprinkle ½ cup onions and 1 stick butter (in chunks) in bottom of roasting pan around chicken. Set aside. Heat oil to 350° and fry potatoes in small batches until beginning to brown but not completely cooked, about 5 minutes. (Adjust heat as needed to maintain temperature at 350°.) Drain on paper towels, then place potatoes in 13" × 9" baking pan. Sprinkle evenly with 1 tablespoon plus 2 teaspoons Seasoning Mix and set aside. In large skillet fry bacon over high heat until brown. Add ham and cook for 3 to 5 minutes, stirring frequently. Stir in remaining 1 cup onions and continue cooking for 5 minutes, stirring occasionally. Remove from heat and using slotted spoon, spoon bacon mixture on top of potatoes. Add stock and 2 tablespoons butter; stir until well mixed. Place pans containing potatoes and reserved chicken in 400° oven and bake until chicken is done, about 35–40 minutes. (Stir potatoes about every 10 minutes.)

Meanwhile, make Cajun Béarnaise Sauce and set aside.

When chicken and potatoes are done, remove pans from oven. Transfer chicken to heated platter and set aside. Spoon potatoes into pan containing chicken drippings and toss potatoes to coat with drippings; set aside. Begin to heat serving plates in 250° oven. In mixing bowl, beat eggs and remaining 2 teaspoons seasoning mix with metal whisk until frothy, about 30 seconds. Melt remaining 4 tablespoons butter in large skillet (preferably nonstick type) over high heat. Add about two thirds of egg mixture to skillet, then use slotted spoon to add potato mixture, and then remaining egg mixture on top of potatoes. Cook until omelette is done. (If preferred, mixture may be scrambled.) Remove from heat and cut omelette into 6 wedges (or divide mixture, if scrambled). Serve immediately.

To serve, place wedge or portion of eggs on each heated serving plate; arrange a "half" chicken on top of eggs, then spoon about ¼ cup of Cajun Béarnaise Sauce over top.

Basic Chicken Stock

10 cups cold water (see Note)

1½ to 2 pounds chicken backs, necks, giblets (excluding liver) and/or bones

1 medium onion, unpeeled, quartered

1 rib celery

1 large clove garlic, unpeeled, quartered

Place all ingredients in large saucepan; bring to boil over high heat, then gently simmer at least 4 hours, preferably 8, replenishing water as needed to keep about 1 quart of liquid in pan. Strain, cool, and refrigerate until ready to use. Makes about 1 quart. Note: Always start with cold water—enough to cover stock ingredients. If short on time, a stock simmered 20 or 30 minutes—in any recipe—is far better than using just water.

Cajun Béarnaise Sauce

1 pound (4 sticks) unsalted butter

6 tablespoons margarine

3 tablespoons plus 2 teaspoons white wine

1 teaspoon dried tarragon leaves

4 egg yolks

2½ teaspoons lemon juice

1 teaspoon Tabasco sauce

1 teaspoon Worcestershire sauce

Melt butter and margarine in 1-quart saucepan over low heat. Raise heat and bring to rapid boil. Remove from heat and cool 5 minutes. Skim froth from top and discard. Pour into large glass measuring cup and set aside. In separate 1-quart saucepan, combine 3 tablespoons of the wine and the tarragon. Cook over high heat until liquid has mostly evaporated (about 2 minutes), stirring occasionally. Let cool 5 minutes. In medium-sized stainless steel mixing bowl or top of double boiler, combine remaining 2 teaspoons wine, cooled tarragon mixture, egg yolks, lemon juice, Tabasco sauce and Worcestershire sauce. Mix together with metal whisk until frothy, about 1 minute. Place bowl over pan of slowly simmering, not boiling, water. (Bowl must never touch water.) Vigorously whisk egg mixture, picking up bowl frequently to let steam escape; whip until egg mixture is very light and creamy and has a sheen, about 5 to 7 minutes. (This amount of beating is important so cooked eggs will hold butter better.) Remove bowl from pan of hot water. Gradually ladle about ¼ cup of the butter mixture (use top butterfat, not butter solids on bottom) into egg mixture while vigorously whipping sauce; make sure each butterfat addition is well mixed into sauce. Continue gradually adding surface butterfat up to a total of approximately 1 cup. To get to butter solids, ladle out and reserve about ½ cup surface butterfat into separate container. (Butter solids add flavor and also thin the sauce.) Gradually ladle all but ⅓ cup of bottom solids into sauce, whisking well. (Use any remaining bottom solids in another dish.) Then gradually whisk in enough of reserved top butterfat to produce a fairly thick sauce. (Butterfat thickens the sauce, so all may not be needed.) Keep sauce in warm place until ready to serve. Makes about 1⅔ cups.

PAUL PRUDHOMME

One of the most acclaimed and certainly the most visible chef in America, he boasts that his ancestors came down from Canada some 200 years ago and settled in the bayou country south of Opelousas. He is the epitome of his own definition of a Cajun— "A Louisianan, an American, and a person who enjoys life to the fullest." He began cooking at the age of seven, helping his mother prepare food for their large family; later served as corporate chef for the Brennans of *Commander's Palace;* then opened, with his wife, K, *K-Paul's Restaurant* on Chartres Street in the French Quarter of New Orleans. In 1984, he published *Chef Paul Prudhomme's Louisiana Kitchen,* containing recipes for his Cajun and Creole creations.

"Cajun food is the methods of the past, the ingredients we have around us, and the fun of food—the spices to make it *alive*— to make your taste buds *cry* for more."

Down Home Brunch

Under a tent on a Charleston plantation or in a backyard in
Shaker Heights, a perfect brunch menu features such down home favorites
as shrimp gumbo, buttermilk biscuits, and pecan pie.
Recipes for these tasty treats are provided, respectively,
by Leontyne Price, Hugh Downs, and Tyne Daly.

POPPY SEED CAKE

¼ cup poppy seeds

1 cup milk

1 cup butter (up to ½ cup
  margarine may be substituted)

¾ cup sugar

2 cups flour

2 teaspoons baking powder

4 egg whites

Soak poppy seeds in milk for several hours. Preheat oven to 325°. Cut butter into pieces and cream with sugar until fluffy. Warm milk mixture slightly, add to creamed butter, and mix well. Sift flour and baking powder and gradually add, mixing well. Beat egg whites until foamy; immediately fold into batter, blending lightly but thoroughly. Turn into buttered bundt or loaf pan. Bake 1 hour or until cake tests done in center. Serves 10.

JOAN BENOIT SAMUELSON

When she won the 1983 Boston Marathon with the best time ever run by a woman, a champion was born. When she captured the gold medal for the first woman's marathon in the 1984 summer Olympic games, a celebrity was born. A quiet, elusive person, she claims her personal appearances demand more of herself than her running and weight training schedule. She lives in the Pine Tree State with her husband Scott.

"I always seem to be running around in circles with very little time to spare — so I like this easy-to-make recipe. It's also a very delicious and light dessert that goes well with fresh fruit or ice cream."

1820

JOAN FLUTIE'S BAKED CORN

2 1 pound cans corn, drained
1 cup cracker crumbs
2 eggs, beaten
Salt and pepper, to taste
1 cup milk
½ cup butter

Preheat oven to 350°. Mix corn, cracker crumbs, eggs, salt, and pepper in large mixing bowl. Heat milk and butter in small saucepan until butter melts. Add milk mixture to corn mixture. Pour into greased casserole dish. Bake about ½ hour or until firm. Serves 6.

DOUG FLUTIE

He was born in The Old Line State in the village of Manchester where the farmlands produce sweet, sweet corn. This gridiron superstar brought instant fame to Boston College with his 48 yard pass in the final moments of a game against arch rival, the Miami Hurricanes. "The Pass" won that game and a berth on the All American team for the spunky 5'9" quarterback. When the Heisman Trophy winner signed with the New Jersey Generals, he became the highest paid rookie in sports history.

"This is my favorite vegetable recipe. Although it is a side dish, I often make it my main course, too!"

GRILLED BUTTERFLIED LAMB WITH TARRAGON

7 to 8 pound leg of lamb
¼ cup oil
Chopped tarragon (at least 3 tablespoons)
1 tablespoon garlic, minced
¼ cup tarragon vinegar
¼ to ½ cup Dijon mustard
4 ounces butter, cut into pats and softened
Freshly ground black pepper, to taste

Have butcher "butterfly" — i.e., debone, open up, and trim — leg of lamb. Put oil in a baking dish and lay lamb out flat in oil. Sprinkle lamb on both sides with chopped tarragon, garlic, tarragon vinegar, Dijon mustard, butter, and pepper. Turn and rub lamb so that it is evenly coated by the marinade. Soak lamb for several hours. Cooking: Place lamb flat on charcoal grill and cook each side 8 to 10 minutes. When cooking is done (this lamb is best served rare), put lamb back in remaining marinade and allow it to remain there for 15 minutes or so before carving. This should do for 6 to 8 guests.

ARTHUR SCHLESINGER, JR.

This *summa cum laude* graduate of Harvard was a member of the Kennedy Administration's "brain trust," serving as the President's special assistant. An analytic and narrative historian, he recorded the history of JFK's thousand days in the White House in a Pulitzer Prize-winning book. Known as an *homme du monde,* he is married to Alexandra Emmet, teaches at City University of New York's graduate school, and writes film critiques as a pastime.

"This recipe has always been a favorite of mine. It is the perfect dish for a summer grill, especially when preceded by a couple of ice cold dry martinis (*not* served on the rocks)."

1788

New England

New England clam chowder, Boston baked beans, Hartford election cake, Vermont maple syrup—no other region has given more place names to its food. Of all the regional fare, perhaps the most favored is Maine lobster. The demand for these feisty crustaceans is so great that more than 15 million are drawn from the icy Down East waters each year.

New England's culinary pride of place had its beginnings when the pilgrims were introduced to native Americans and their sustenance—wild turkeys and cranberries, corn, squash, and beans. Maine lobsters were abundant as were oysters and scallops. There were blueberries and wild grapes and the tart beach plum that rimmed the Cape Cod coast. For greens, the colonists took to dandelions and fiddlehead ferns. The beneficent climate and excellent soil also welcomed the seeds and saplings brought across the ocean from the old country.

The new Americans used their budding Yankee ingenuity to good cookery advantage. Trees were tapped; maple syrup was invented. Potash was used as the earliest form of baking powder. Cornmeal was glorified in a dozen delicious dishes. Best of all, New Englanders turned a lowly combination of crust and apples into the great American favorite—apple pie.

MARTHA STEWART

Leaving behind successful careers as model and stockbroker, she moved to Connecticut to undertake the renovation of a 19th century farmhouse and gardens—and launched another successful career as caterer. *Entertaining* and her series of cookbooks have sold millions of copies and have made her one of America's most famous hostesses.

"My corner of Connecticut, with its barns, gardens and orchards, chickens and turkeys, clamming flats and lobster pots, is a microcosm of the world of New England with its extravagant gifts from the sea and produce from the land. Today, New Englanders are rediscovering the pleasure of grapes from the neighbor's vines, honey from the local beehive, herbs from the kitchen garden, and incredible home grown vegetables for the table."

CHICKEN "CHAN"

1 6 to 8 pound roasting chicken

½ cup dry white wine

1 10½ ounce can beef broth

1 stick butter or margarine

1 teaspoon dried tarragon

Salt, to taste

2 celery stalks with leaves

2 carrots

1 onion, peeled

1 clove garlic, optional

Clean chicken both inside and out. (Remember to wash your hands after.) Towel dry. (Chicken, *not* your hands.) Place chicken in roasting pan. Pour on wine and ½ cup of beef broth. Marinate in refrigerator for several hours. Remove chicken from fridge a good hour before putting it in the oven. Dab chicken with butter or margarine and sprinkle with tarragon and a little salt. In the cavity, place the carrots, celery, onion, and garlic. Preheat oven, then set to 350° Roast for 2 to 2½ hours, basting often with pan juice and remaining beef broth. Serves 4.

CHARLOTTE FORD AND ANNE FORD SCARBOROUGH

They were born with silver spoons in their mouths, and their dazzling debut party was covered by *Life* magazine, but these close sisters, daughters of Henry Ford II, are active women, involved in charitable and community service. Charlotte entered the fashion field designing a dress and sportswear collection, which was a rousing financial success. She has written a best-selling etiquette book, *Charlotte Ford's Book of Modern Manners,* and teaches etiquette classes to high school youngsters in Manhattan and the Bronx. Anne serves on the boards of The Gateway School and "Resources," organizations devoted to children with special needs. Married to broadcast journalist Chuck Scarborough, she has continued her education at the New School and is currently enrolled at Hunter College, studying economics and international politics.

"Grandfather helped put a car in every garage. With this recipe, we hope to put a chicken in every pot."

1837

WILD RICE CASSEROLE

1½ cups wild rice
3 tablespoons butter
¼ cup chopped onion
1 cup sliced, fresh mushrooms
1 cup chopped celery
Pinch of sage
Pinch of thyme
1 can condensed cream of mushroom soup
Salt and pepper, to taste

Soak rice in water overnight. Drain. Place in saucepan, cover with 2″ to 3″ water and boil slowly, covered, until rice is well-puffed — about 30 minutes. Melt butter in skillet and sauté onions, mushrooms, and celery 3 to 5 minutes or until vegetables wilt. Drain rice but do not blanch. Combine rice and vegetables, then add sage, thyme, mushroom soup, salt and pepper. Mix together, transfer to 3 quart casserole, and bake 20 minutes in 300° oven. Serves 6.

Editor's note: Peter Graves says this serves 6. We think it serves 12 but hesitate to disagree with this 6′3″ *Mission: Impossible* agent.

PETER GRAVES

After a stint in the Air Force, this native son of Minneapolis studied drama at the University of Minnesota, then headed for Hollywood where he quickly found a niche in Westerns, as did his brother James Arness, the sheriff of *Gunsmoke*. Tall, ruggedly handsome, and with a commanding voice, he was a dashing member of the cast of the long-running *Mission: Impossible* television series.

   "The wild rice casserole was a traditional dish used by the early Norwegian and German settlers of Minnesota. Delicious served with wild duck."

SHRIMP GUMBO

½ cup chopped onion

5 tablespoons butter (divided)

3 tablespoons flour

4½ cups chicken broth

1 20 ounce can tomatoes

Salt, to taste

2 teaspoons minced parsley

¼ teaspoon thyme

1 clove garlic, minced

2 bay leaves

2 cups cooked okra (fresh or frozen)

1 teaspoon gumbo filé powder

18 shrimp, peeled and deveined

8 ounces crab meat

Hot cooked rice

In large skillet, sauté onion in 2 tablespoons of the butter for 5 minutes. Add remaining butter. When melted, blend in flour. Add broth, stirring until smooth. Add tomatoes, salt, parsley, thyme, garlic, and bay leaves to sauce. Cover and simmer 1 hour. Add okra, filé powder, shrimp, and crab meat and simmer 8 to 10 minutes longer. Serve over hot, cooked rice. Serves 6.

LEONTYNE PRICE

From *diva di tutti le dive* to *prima donna assoluta* to "the Stradivarius of singers," there is not an accolade that has not been accorded this soprano. She soared to fame with her performance of Bess in Gershwin's *Porgy and Bess.* Her debut as Leonora in *Il Trovatore* at the Metropolitan Opera received a 42 minute ovation. Her numerous awards include America's highest, the Presidential Medal of Freedom, plus 18 Grammys and three Emmys, and she was chosen to open the new Metropolitan Opera House at New York's Lincoln Center as the lead in Samuel Barber's *Antony and Cleopatra.* Born in the Magnolia state, she now lives in a Federal house in Greenwich Village, New York.

"My father's eyes always had an extra glow when my mother brought this delicious dish steaming hot to the table on Sunday after church. I hope you will enjoy it as well. Good appetite!"

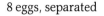

DARK AND DANGEROUS CHOCOLATE CAKE

8 eggs, separated

8 ounces butter

8 ounces unsweetened dark chocolate

2 cups unrefined sugar

¾ cup breadcrumbs

2 tablespoons *Grand Marnier*

Grated peel of 1 orange

Preheat oven to 375°. Melt butter with chocolate without boiling. Mix sugar with melted butter and chocolate in a bowl. Add egg yolks one by one while stirring into mixture. Add breadcrumbs, *Grand Marnier,* and grated orange peel and mix well. Beat egg whites until stiff and fold into batter. Pour into greased 10″ pan. Bake for 15 minutes at 375°, then lower oven to 350° and continue baking for ¾ hour. Serve with hot raspberries and/or vanilla ice cream.

JOHN HUSTON AND ANJELICA HUSTON

John Huston was born in Nevada, Missouri. Now an octogenarian, the recipient of the American Film Institute's prestigious Lifetime Achievement Award said recently he was finally getting the hang of making movies. As actor, he has appeared in a wide range of roles from hairy ape in *Battle of the Planet of the Apes* to Noah in *The Bible.* The first movie he directed was *The Maltese Falcon* with Humphrey Bogart; later he directed his father, the beloved actor Walter Huston, in *The Treasure of the Sierra Madres.* Carrying on the Huston theatrical tradition in typical grand style for a third generation, daughter Anjelica recently won the Oscar for Best Supporting Actress for her role in *Prizzi's Honor. Harper's Bazaar* magazine has just picked her as one of the 10 most beautiful women in America.

Classic
Dining

Evenings that call for china and crystal require an
equally elegant menu. We propose, to start, pumpkin soup Dave Brubeck,
followed by grilled butterflied lamb Arthur Schlesinger, jr.,
and wild rice Peter Graves. Add a color coordinated
salad and some fresh New Jersey asparagus and finish on a light
note with Dina Merrill's apricot mousse.

MY BROTHER-IN-LAW TOM PICK'S BARBECUE SAUCE

½ cup ketchup

½ cup white sugar

4 tablespoons vinegar

4 tablespoons water

3 tablespoons butter, melted

3 tablespoons brown sugar

2 tablespoons Worcestershire sauce

2 tablespoons honey

1 tablespoon lemon juice

1 tablespoon chili powder

1 teaspoon English Pub (stone ground) mustard

1 teaspoon paprika

1 teaspoon salt

½ teaspoon black pepper

Approximately 2 teaspoons Heinz Seafood Cocktail Sauce

Mix all ingredients together. Spread on chicken. Grill over moderate heat, basting well and turning for 1 hour or more. Makes 2 cups sauce.

GLENN CLOSE

A New Englander by birth, a New Yorker by residence, and a Montanan by inclination, this aristocratic actress traces her family roots in this country to 1682. Who would have expected that this lyric soprano who sang the national anthem at Mets' games in Shea Stadium would go on to win a Tony Award for best actress in *The Real Thing,* be twice nominated for an academy award, and knock Broadway dead with her performance in *Benefactors.* Her acting success could have been predicted by her classmates at Rosemary Hall where she organized a theatre troupe called *The Fingernails — The Group with Polish.*

1889

POPCORN

I was born in Gibbon in the Cornhusker State. I don't cook but I make a mean popcorn. Although popcorn may be made over an open fire using a wire popper or in a microwave oven using a special utensil, serious connoisseurs do it over a stove using a heavy-lidded, heavy pot. Heat 1 tablespoon peanut oil in pot over moderate heat. (To get the flavor of movie theatre popcorn, use cocoanut oil.) Sprinkle ¼ cup kernels evenly on bottom of pot. Cover tightly and shake steadily until popping subsides. Toss with melted butter and season with salt. Each ¼ cup of kernels makes about 1 pint popcorn — enough for a cartoon or a short feature. To eat properly, flick the popcorn from the wrist and chew with mouth open.

Editor's note: Quadequina, the Indian chief, brought popcorn to the Pilgrim's first Thanksgiving feast in 1621. After that it became a token of good will, often presented at peace talks between colonists and Indians. Early Indians believed a tiny demon inside each kernel made them pop. In 1871, a Chicagoan mixed up popcorn with molasses and peanuts and dubbed it Crackerjack, which became immortalized in the song, *Take Me Out to the Ballgame.* Today it is possible to buy popcorn in at least 60 flavors, ranging from watermelon to chocolate. There is even such a delicacy as whiskey sour popcorn balls. Unadorned, popcorn, which is high in protein, phosphorous, iron, and fiber, is rumored to be popular diet food. But most of us like it drenched with melted butter, the way President Ronald Reagan, a big popcorn fancier, serves it at White House screenings.

DICK CAVETT

Broadway actor, comedian, writer, award-winning magician, gymnast, and enthusiastic tap dancer, he records all these interests and more in two autobiographical books, *Cavett* and *Eye on Cavett.* The only child of teachers, he has a lively curiosity and colorful style of interviewing that over the years have won him Emmy awards as well as a large, loyal audience.

43

NEVADA ★★★★★★★★

NEVADA BASQUE LENTEN PIE

1 cup chopped onions

⅔ cup chopped green peppers

4 cloves garlic, minced

3 tablespoons oil

1 28 ounce can tomatoes

1 6 ounce can tomato paste

Salt and pepper, to taste

6 eggs

In a large, heavy frying pan, sauté onions, green peppers, and garlic in oil until tender. Add tomatoes and tomato paste. Add salt and pepper, to taste. Partially cover and simmer slowly, stirring occasionally, about 1 hour. Pour mixture into a 9″×9″ baking pan (or leave in iron skillet if it is ovenproof). Carefully break 6 eggs individually into mixture. Place pan in a 350° oven and bake until eggs are set. Serves 6.

Variation
Hard cooked eggs cut into wedges may be substituted. In which case, the eggs are placed on a warm platter, the sauce is poured over, and the pie is served immediately.

SENATOR PAUL LAXALT

His parents were both from the Basque region of France. His father, Dominique, was a successful sheepman. His mother, Teresa, a Cordon Bleu graduate, went to Nevada to visit a dying brother, met Dominique and never returned to her homeland. And in this land of opportunity, their son grew up to become Governor. He is now Senator, a close friend and advisor to President Reagan, and rumored to be a future presidential candidate.

"This recipe reflects the heritage of the thousands of Basques from the Pyrenees of France and Spain who settled in the deserts and mountains of the American West—especially Nevada. Because Basques are predominantly Catholic, this recipe for the Lenten season is most appropriate."

1864

NEW ENGLAND CLAM CHOWDER

Neophytes to the ways of chowder (pronounced chowdah) beware: the following recipe makes a whole lot of this most life-giving soup, the only amount to make, as one can be sociable and share its glories with friends, or one can (as I often do) hoard it and have it day after day. If you must, you may halve the ingredients. You won't next time. One of the truths of chowder is that it only gets better with reheatings. Like a true New Englander, it gains character and strength over time. I will not pause here to distinguish this food of gods from that reddish bracken served in some depraved urban areas to the south. As it is written: *"Don't mix bivalves with bay leaves!"*

4 dozen quahogs

½ pound salt pork, finely chopped or minced

5 peeled Russet potatoes, chopped

2 large white onions, peeled and chopped

2 quarts half and half or plain milk

1 clove garlic

1 cup cream

Butter, as desired

Pepper, to taste

Once you've established that there are no bay leaves anywhere near your cooking surfaces or, even in the house, you're ready. If you don't have a clam steamer (yet), place the rinsed quahogs in a large pot with 2" of water, and cover. With heat on high, let them steam *just* until they open, stirring occasionally to rotate bottom clams to top. As the quahogs open, take them out, letting juice drip back into pot. Remove meat from shells and place on chopping board. Place shells in sink. Chop excess stuffs from clams, leaving only central, meaty part. Place excess stuffs back. Add 6 cups of water and clam shells. Chop clams into bite size pieces and place in

small skillet with thin covering of water. Bring to simmer, reduce heat to low, and cover. Meanwhile, in another skillet, fry salt pork, onions, and pressed garlic clove, stirring frequently, until onions are translucent. Set aside. Place potatoes into small amount of boiling water in large pot. Simmer 7 to 8 minutes and drain. Add contents of skillets (clams and pork) together with half and half or milk and 2 cups of clam broth from the other pot. A baster is a handy implement with which to get at the broth. Cover and cook on low for an hour or two so that ingredients have time to get acquainted. Add cream, butter, and pepper just before serving.

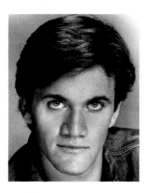

MATT SALINGER

He made his stage debut in the third grade as a mouse soldier in a school production of *The Nutcracker* and by the time he was a prep school senior he had progressed to leading roles. He graduated from Columbia University before "going on the boards." He's remembered as the overly amorous lacrosse player in *One Life to Live* and as a football jock in *Revenge of the Nerds.* He recently co-starred in the television mini-series *Blood and Orchids.* In an accomplished family, his mother is a Jungian psychologist; his sister an Oxford scholar; and his father the writer J. D. Salinger.

"For festive occasions like a Red Sox sweep of the Yankees, I suggest laying in a few six packs of Haffenreffer beer to go with the chowdah."

45

SARA'S SOUP

1 tablespoon grated onions

2 tablespoons butter

1 package of frozen peas
(preferably small size peas)

1 10½ ounce can beef consommé

1 tablespoon brown sugar

2 teaspoons thyme

Pinch garlic salt

1 cup heavy cream

Split of champagne

Brown onions in butter. Add peas, consommé, sugar, thyme, and garlic salt and cook until peas are unfrozen (about 10 minutes) but not longer. Cool slightly. Add heavy cream to mixture and place in blender or food processor. Blend thoroughly. Refrigerate at least 24 hours. Divide a split of champagne into 4 cups and fill up with soup. Serves 4.

FREDERICA VON STADE

Born in the Garden State into a prominent family, she is nicknamed "Flicka" after one of her father's polo ponies. A mezzo-soprano, she made her international debut in 1973 in Paris as Cherubino in the *Marriage of Figaro*. Since then, she has sung in every major opera house in Europe and the United States and won the Grand Prix du Disque in 1982 for her recording of *Chants d'Auvergne*.

"I call this Sara's soup after my mother from whom I inherited the recipe."

The Mid-Atlantic

All five of the Mid-Atlantic states—New York, New Jersey, Delaware, Pennsylvania, and Maryland—were among the Thirteen Colonies, and many old and prized farmlands are established there. Despite its reputation for industry, New Jersey is a leading state in farm income per acre. In the southern portion, a profusion of vegetables grow, especially tomatoes and asparagus. New York, too, is rich agriculturally. Crisscrossing the chic, weekend communities of the Hamptons on eastern Long Island are dusty potato farms. Apple orchards and vineyards carpet the Finger Lakes region, and dairy farms are so widespread that the state ranks second only to Wisconsin as a milk producer. In the Great Valley, the Pennsylvania Dutch have built a culture that is identified with the bountiful agrarian life. Little Delaware, known as the Diamond State because of its carat size and its precious soil, is rich in farmlands yielding corn, grains, and potatoes. And while Maryland may be best known for its catch of fish and shellfish from the Chesapeake Bay, it contains acres of fertile farmland. The legacy of the original states is rich, indeed.

MICHAEL AND ARIANE BATTERBERRY

Michael and Ariane Batterberry are authors of numerous bestsellers in the fields of food, art, and social history. They co-founded *Food and Wine* magazine and have recently completed a major cultural history of American regional cuisines.

"The Mid-Atlantic states were the first to light the kitchen fire under America's melting pot. They welcomed the settlers from the European continent and absorbed each new wave of old country recipes with relish. Dutch traders in New York opened their port to French Huguenots, Danes, Spaniards, Italians, and Jews. In Pennsylvania, English Quakers were joined by Dutch and German immigrants of like conscience. Swedes put down roots in Delaware, while the Scottish and Irish fanned out across the entire area. As a result, Americans soon became familiar with mashed potatoes, buckwheat cakes and oatmeal cookies, waffles and cream cheese, noodles and doughnuts, to rattle off only a few.

"New York City, Philadelphia, and Washington, D.C., in turn, served as the young republic's capitol, which obliged each to play official host to the cosmopolitan crowds of ambassadors and enterprising foreign business venturers that descended upon them. In sophisticated Mid-Atlantic circles, French chefs, confectioners, and wine merchants were to become as familiar as indentured hands, fruit pedlars, and oystermen had been. Today New York City still represents the culinary clearinghouse and test kitchen for the country, where more different cuisines may be sampled than any other place in the world."

ENCHILADA CASSEROLE

1 pound ground beef

3 cans condensed cream of chicken soup

4 4 ounce cans chopped green chilies, drained

1½ soup cans of milk

1 package flour tortillas

1 pound grated Longhorn cheese, approximately

Brown ground beef in skillet and drain all grease. In another pot, combine soup and green chilies. Gradually add milk. Simmer until sauce is smooth, stirring occasionally. Cover bottom of an 8″ × 10″ casserole with sauce and set remainder aside. Warm tortillas in foil in a slow oven until soft — you do not want the tortillas crispy! Spread out tortillas and place a heaping tablespoon of beef and cheese on each. Roll tortilla *tightly* and place in casserole. You now have an enchilada! Continue rolling tortillas, tucking snugly into pan. Pour remaining sauce over enchiladas. Make sure to put sauce in between enchiladas so they stay moist. Sprinkle remaining cheese on top. Bake at 350° for approximately 30 minutes. Serves 6 to 8.

NANCY LOPEZ

Golf pro Nancy Lopez may have had the most spectacular debut in the history of organized sports. In her first full year on the LPGA tour, 1978, she won nine tournaments and was named both Rookie and Player of the Year. She has been piling up titles, record-setting performances, and earnings ever since. Now a mother of two, this young Mexican-American gives a lot of credit to the support she received from her family. Her father, Domingo, got her out on the course when she was seven, and 13 years later she dedicated herself to winning her first pro tournament in memory of her mother.

"As a child I used to make this dish with my mother. We used all fresh ingredients and actually picked the chilies ourselves. The recipe can also be made with one pound of boiled, shredded chicken in place of the ground beef."

1912

PASTA PRIMAVERA

2 tablespoons olive oil

2 tablespoons butter

¼ pound mushrooms, washed and sliced

1 small zucchini, sliced

8 asparagus tips

¼ pound snow peas, trimmed

2 cloves garlic, mashed

¼ cup white wine

½ pound angel hair pasta

½ cup homemade chicken stock

Salt and freshly ground pepper, to taste

Parmesan cheese, freshly grated

Heat oil and butter in a pan. Add mushrooms and zucchini and toss until very well coated. Add asparagus and snow peas. Toss over high heat but do not let brown. Add garlic and wine. Cook for 30 seconds to reduce slightly. (At this point begin to cook pasta in boiling water.) Add chicken stock and simmer 1 minute. Season with salt and pepper. Add Parmesan cheese, to taste. Drain pasta when cooked *al dente.* Combine with sauce and toss over heat. Add more Parmesan, to taste. Serve very hot in a large bowl. Serves 4.

MAYOR EDWARD I. KOCH

"How'm I doing?" is the familiar motto of The Big Apple mayor whose popularity matches that of the late Fiorello La Guardia. Born in the Bronx to Polish immigrant parents, he was educated at New York University and practiced law in Greenwich Village before commencing his three mayoral terms. He frequently retreats from his formal digs at Gracie Mansion to his modest, one-bedroom Village apartment. "Hiz Honor" is a notorious gourmand.

"It's no secret that I love good food. This particular recipe for Pasta Primavera is my absolute favorite — the best pasta dish I've ever had. The key is to serve it hot and not spare the garlic. It's especially great accompanied by a glass of New York State wine. Enjoy!"

1788

49

RAGGEDY ANN© SALAD

Ingredients for each salad

1 canned pear half

1 scoop cottage cheese

½ cup shredded carrot

Pitted black olives

Paprika

Carrots and celery sticks

Pimento

Lettuce

Arrange pear half on individual salad plate. Place scoop of cottage cheese above to make Raggedy Ann's head. Cut end from pitted olive and slice remainder into rings. Use two olive rings for eyes, piece of pimento for nose, and a smaller piece for center of mouth. Strips cut from end of olive form the "smile." Paprika makes dandy cheeks. Arrange shredded carrot around cottage cheese for hair. Use carrot sticks to form arms and celery sticks to form legs. An olive cut in half lengthwise forms feet. A frill of lettuce leaf makes a pretty skirt. Remaining olive slices can be used as buttons.

RAGGEDY ANN©
AND RAGGEDY ANDY

As American as apple pie, Raggedy Ann was created in 1918 by cartoonist and illustrator Johnny Gruelle. Two years later, she was joined by a little rag brother, Raggedy Andy. Together, these soft, floppy rag dolls have been beloved both by children and adults. Johnny Gruelle's son, Worth, illustrated the Raggedy Ann stories after his father's death in 1939. His other son, Richard, appears as the character "Dickie" in some of the Raggedy Ann stories. Both Richard and Worth Gruelle have homes in North Carolina. The Raggedy Ann dolls and the recipe for Raggedy Ann Salad are courtesy of collector Jonathan Green.

Raggedy Ann says, "It tickles me to think of the lovely ladies' luncheons in the 1920s when this salad doll was served. Nowadays, I like it as a treat for good little boys and girls when I hostess tea parties in the nursery."

© 1985 Macmillan, Inc.

1789

CHICKEN AND DUMPLINGS

3 whole chicken breasts

3 chicken backs

1 carrot, coarsely chopped

2 stalks celery, coarsely chopped

1 medium onion, coarsely chopped

Place chicken breasts in kettle, cover with approximately 1½ quarts cool water and bring to boil. Simmer, covered, 20 minutes or until tender. Remove chicken breasts and set aside. (When cooled, remove bones and skin.) Add chicken backs, carrot, celery, and onion to broth. Simmer 30 minutes. Strain broth and set aside.

Sauce

1 stick butter or margarine

½ cup flour

2 tablespoons dry sherry

Juice of ½ lemon

Salt and white pepper, to taste

Melt butter. Add flour and beat until smooth. Stir in 5 cups strained broth and cook over low heat for 5 minutes. Add sherry, lemon juice, salt and pepper.

Dumplings

1½ cups flour

2 teaspoons baking powder

¼ teaspoon salt

3 tablespoons shortening

¾ cup milk

Nutmeg, freshly grated

Mix flour, baking powder, and salt. Cut in shortening until mixture looks like cornmeal. Stir in milk until well blended. Cover a steamer rack with lightly oiled waxed paper. Set rack in pan 2 to 3 inches above ½ inch of boiling water. Drop batter from spoon onto paper. Steam dumplings 8 minutes uncovered, then 10 minutes with lid on. To serve, place dumplings on top chicken breasts with sauce poured over all. Dust with nutmeg. Serves 6.

LAWRENCE WELK

Before his 16-year stint on prime time television, he conducted the Honolulu Fruit Gum Chewing Orchestra. The celebrity you can take home to grandmother, he is as committed to wholesomeness as a state fair organizer. Born in Strasburg, North Dakota, he tells the story of his bubbling life in *Wunnerful, Wunnerful* and *Ah-One, Ah-Two*. His license plate: A1ANDA2!

OHIO ★★★★★★★★

BUCKEYE BUTTERMILK BISCUITS

1¾ cups flour

½ teaspoon salt

2 teaspoons baking powder

½ teaspoon baking soda

4 tablespoons butter

6 strips crisp bacon, crumbled

¾ cup buttermilk, approximately

Cheddar cheese, optional

Preheat oven to 425°. Sift (or stir well) together flour, salt, baking powder, and baking soda. Cut in butter with two knives (or use a food processor or fingertips) until the mixture resembles coarse meal. Toss in bacon. Lightly stir in just enough milk to make a soft dough. Have ready a floured board. Turn dough onto it and pat lightly to ½" thickness. Cut into a dozen 2" squares. Place on buttered baking tin. Bake immediately 12 minutes or until tops are lightly browned. For a toothsome treat, split hot biscuits and tuck a wedge of cheese into each.

HUGH DOWNS

He insists he's a television "guest," not a "host," that *he's* the one coming into people's homes. By that rule, he's been in billions of living rooms via his stints on *The Tonight Show, Today*, quiz shows, and his present spot on *20/20*. He has been broadcasting for an amazing 47 years— beginning as an 18 year-old announcer at radio station WLOK in Lima, Ohio.

MUSKINGUM CHOCOLATE DEW CAKE

2 cups cake flour

1 cup sugar

4 tablespoons cocoa

½ teaspoon salt

2 teaspoons baking soda

1 cup cold water

1 cup mayonnaise or salad dressing

1 teaspoon vanilla

Preheat oven to 350°. Sift together several times, cake flour, sugar, cocoa, salt, and baking soda. Thoroughly mix water and mayonnaise or salad dressing together. Combine the 2 mixtures. Add vanilla and mix well. Pour into 2 buttered 8" cake pans. Bake ½ hour and test with toothpick for doneness. Frost with a chocolate icing. Serves 10.

SENATOR JOHN GLENN

His father had hoped he would take over the family heating and plumbing business, but his first flying lesson, while a sophomore at Muskingum College, was to launch him into other orbits. As a World War II marine, he was decorated 17 times; as a military test pilot, he made the first nonstop transcontinental supersonic flight. When he was honored at a joint session of Congress as the first American to orbit the earth in a space capsule (Friendship 7), the patriot endeared himself to the world when he unexpectedly introduced his wife with these simple words: "This is Annie— I'm real proud of her."

"This is the cake our children ordered made on special occasions such as birthdays. I like moist cakes—and with a chocolate icing, this one can't be beaten."

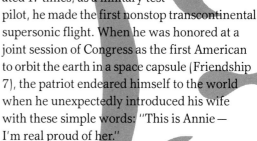

TONY'S MOTHER'S POTATOES

Everyone thinks that because I played Felix I can cook, but I'm lucky if I can soft boil an egg. There is one thing, however, that I really know how to make because my mother served it all the time when we were growing up in Oklahoma. You take little red potatoes and boil them in their jackets. That's important — that you boil them in their jackets. You slice them into half-inch slices. Put a goodly amount of butter into a skillet with some diced onions. Brown the potatoes in the butter. Serve with skillet drippings poured over the potatoes.

TONY RANDALL

He has played Shakespeare and Shaw but will ever be remembered for his Emmy winning role as the fussy, ashtray emptying bachelor Felix Unger in the television series *The Odd Couple.* In real life, he is married to his childhood sweetheart Florence Mitchell. A passionate opera buff, he is as much at home hosting *Live from Lincoln Center* broadcasts as he is raconteuring on talk shows. He is Chairman of the Myasthenia Gravis Foundation.

"I didn't care, growing up, if I had nothing else for dinner but my mother's potatoes."

1907

Tex-Mex Saturday Night

Specialties of the Southwest, with their spicy, south-of-the-border accents, are to the 80s what ham and potato salad were to an earlier time— great crowd pleasers and prepare-ahead fare for a jeans clad group on a weekend night. For a hot combination, serve up Polly Bergen's Chili for a Crowd, Erma Bombeck's Layered Ranchero Dip, Malcolm Forbes' Trinchera Tacos, and Nancy Lopez's Enchilada Casserole.

OREGON ★★★★★★★

PORTLAND PEACH PIE

2 cups milk

2 eggs

½ cup sugar

3 tablespoons cornstarch

Dash of salt

½ teaspoon vanilla

1 tablespoon butter

4 to 6 peaches

8″ graham cracker crust

Whipped cream

In medium saucepan, mix milk and eggs with beater. Combine sugar, cornstarch, and salt in bowl. Slowly add dry mixture to egg mixture, stirring with wooden spoon. Cook over medium heat, stirring constantly, until mixture boils and thickens. Take from heat and add vanilla and butter. Stir and let cool. Peel and slice peaches just before use (to prevent discoloring) and arrange in crust. Pour cooled mixture over peaches. Cover with whipped cream and store in refrigerator until set. Serves 6 to 8.

SALLY STRUTHERS

Living proof that good things come in small packages, this petite actress has never been typecast. She believably created Gloria, the ingenious daughter of Archie Bunker on television's *All in the Family* and Jack Nicholson's knowing bowling alley pick-up in the film *Five Easy Pieces.* On Broadway, she starred in *Wally's Cafe* with Rita Moreno and James Coco and in the flipside version of *The Odd Couple.* Since 1973, she has been vitally involved with the Christian Children's Foundation, the world's oldest and largest child welfare organization.

"Not too many people think of peaches when they think of Portland—it's usually apples that get the press! But we had two huge peach trees in our backyard, and every year I couldn't wait for the peaches to ripen so I could help Mother Struthers make her famous peach pies."

1859

PENNSYLVANIA ★ ★ ★ ★ ★

PENNSYLVANIA RAISIN AND ORANGE STUFFED GAME HENS

2 Cornish game hens

Salt and pepper

2 corn muffins, crumbled

¼ cup raisins

1 teaspoon grated orange rind

¼ cup butter, melted (divided)

1 6 ounce can frozen orange juice concentrate, thawed (divided)

⅛ teaspoon cloves

⅛ teaspoon ginger

Preheat oven to 375°. Rinse hens and dry. Sprinkle inside and out with salt and pepper. In bowl, combine muffins, raisins, orange rind, half of the melted butter, and ¼ cup of orange juice concentrate. Spoon into hens, skewer closed. Place on rack in shallow pan. Combine remaining butter, remaining orange juice concentrate, cloves, and ginger and brush over hens. Roast (brushing with glaze and turning every 15 minutes) for 1 hour. Split to serve. Serves 4.

MARY EMMERLING

Home furnishings designer, author, decorator, and shopkeeper, she identified the American Country look in decorating and showed the nation how to express it with tin toys, oil lamps, quilts, and duck decoys. Her two books on the subject, *American Country* and *Collecting American Country*, have each sold over 100 thousand copies. A great great granddaughter of President William Henry Harrison, she explores the influences on American design of Indian, Mexican, European, and cowboy traditions in her latest work *American Country West.*

"Perhaps nowhere in the United States is the American Country way of life more a totality than in Pennsylvania with its rich Pennsylvania Dutch and Central European heritage. Shunpiking through the back roads of Bucks County for antiques is a favorite pastime."

1787

PUMPKIN SOUP

2 tablespoons butter or margarine

¼ cup chopped onion

1½ teaspoons curry powder

1 tablespoon flour

2 cups cooked pumpkin pulp
  (preferably steamed fresh)

1 teaspoon brown sugar

⅛ teaspoon nutmeg or mace

⅛ teaspoon cayenne pepper

3 cups chicken broth

2½ cups cream or 2 12 ounce cans
  evaporated milk

Salt

Sour cream or yoghurt

Parsley, watercress or chives, minced

Melt butter or margarine in a 4 quart heavy saucepan. Sauté onion, curry powder, and flour for 2 to 3 minutes, being careful not to burn. Run pumpkin, brown sugar, nutmeg or mace, and cayenne pepper through a food processor (or through a blender a little at a time), adding some chicken broth for moisture. Transfer pumpkin mixture and remainder of broth to butter mixture, stirring thoroughly while bringing it to a simmer. Add cream or evaporated milk and bring to a simmer again. Taste to adjust spices. Add salt if needed or additional pepper. If too spicy add more milk. Serve with a dollop of sour cream or yoghurt in each bowl. Garnish with minced parsley, watercress, or chives. Serves 6.

DAVE BRUBECK

Pianist, composer, and performer, Dave Brubeck has pressed jazz music to the limits for nearly 40 years. His classic album, *Time Out,* with its unorthodox time signatures and daring harmonics, was the first modern jazz album to sell over one million copies. While performing nearly 100 concerts a year, he has also taken time out to compose some 250 pieces including symphonic arrangements and sacred music. In addition to constant globe-trotting, the Dave Brubeck Quartet has been a more than 30 year tradition at the star spangled Newport Jazz Festival.

"Last fall I had a bumper crop of pumpkins in my garden. We had pumpkin pies, baked pumpkin, pumpkin bread, but the favorite was pumpkin soup, which we served at Christmas dinner. It was so delicious we almost forgot about the turkey to follow. My wife is an improviser in the kitchen, just as I am at the piano, but this is how we remember the recipe."

1790

CHARLESTON EGG BALLS

8 hard boiled eggs, cooled

½ cup butter

1 teaspoon salt

¼ teaspoon red pepper

½ teaspoon Worcestershire sauce

¼ teaspoon celery seed

1 cup bread crumbs

With an electric mixer or food processor, cream eggs and butter until well blended. Add salt, pepper, Worcestershire sauce, and celery seed and blend. Refrigerate several hours. Form mixture into 1″ balls, then roll in bread crumbs. Makes 30 balls. May be frozen.

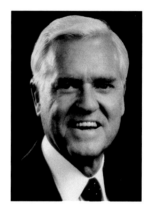

SENATOR ERNEST HOLLINGS

Born in the Palmetto State on New Year's Day, he attended The Citadel and earned a law degree from the University of South Carolina. Formerly governor of his home state, today he is one of the Deep South's most powerful senators. Day care centers, higher pay for teachers, and protection of the environment are issues that have benefitted from his attention during three decades of public service. He is popularly known as "Fritz," and as the third member of the budget triumvirate, Gramm-Rudman-Hollings.

"My wife 'Peatsy' says that, 'Since butter is used instead of mayonnaise there is less chance of spoiling. This was important in the warm climate of Charleston, South Carolina, prior to refrigeration and air conditioning. This is a recipe that has been passed down through the generations.' "

SOUTH DAKOTA ★★★★

RAW APPLE CAKE

1 cup shortening

2 cups sugar

2 eggs

2 tart apples, pared and chopped

1 cup chopped pecans or walnuts

1 cup golden raisins

3 cups flour

2 teaspoons cinnamon

1 teaspoon cloves

2 teaspoons baking soda

1 cup very strong, cold coffee

Preheat oven to 350° Cream shortening and sugar thoroughly in very large bowl. Beat in eggs, one at a time. Stir in apples, nuts, and raisins. Sift together flour, cinnamon, cloves, and baking soda. Mix creamed mixture and flour mixture alternately with coffee. Turn into 9" × 13" greased baking pan. Bake 50 to 60 minutes or until pick inserted into center comes out dry. Serves 16 or more.

CHERYL LADD

1889

Born appropriately in the Sunshine State, this sunny blonde made her show business debut at the age of seven in a hometown (Russell) dance recital. In high school, touring with the Huron school band, she "made it to Hollywood." She is remembered for her role in *Charlie's Angels* when she joined the cast upon the departure of Farah Fawcett. In the year following, three million Cheryl Ladd posters were sold. She has starred in numerous television plays, including the Princess Grace story on ABC. She serves as Ambassador-at-Large to Childhelp U.S.A.

"It's an old fashioned spice cake that needs no icing. Great for breakfast!"

TENNESSEE ★★★★★★

CHILI FOR A CROWD

3 cloves garlic, minced

Oil for browning

6 large onions, finely chopped

6 large green peppers, finely chopped

6 pounds ground round or chuck

5 16 ounce cans Italian-style tomatoes

2 6 ounce cans tomato paste

4 to 6 16 ounce cans kidney beans, drained

2 teaspoons wine vinegar

5 whole cloves

3 bay leaves

4 tablespoons chili powder, or more, to taste

4 drops Tabasco sauce, or to taste

2 teaspoons cumin

Sugar, to taste

Salt and pepper, to taste

In large roasting pan, sauté garlic in oil, remove and reserve. In same pan, sauté onions and peppers until golden; remove, drain, and reserve. Brown meat; drain fat. Return garlic, onions, and peppers to pan and mix well with meat. Add next 9 ingredients. Season to taste with sugar, salt, and pepper. Cover and simmer for 1 hour. Simmer, uncovered, for 1 hour longer. Remove cloves and bay leaves before serving. Serves 25.

POLLY BERGEN

She started as a country singer, then moved into pop music, movies, and finally television, where she crescendoed her way to an Emmy in *The Helen Morgan Story*. For years, she marketed a line of cosmetics before selling it to Faberge. Born in Knoxville, she was the first woman elected to the board of the Singer Company.

"I love this recipe for buffets. Served with a salad and bread, it makes a hearty meal."

SOUTHERN SPOON BREAD

2 cups milk

1 cup white cornmeal

4 eggs, separated

¼ cup butter, cut into pieces

1 tablespoon sugar

½ teaspoon salt

Butter

Preheat oven to 375°. Scald milk in a heavy saucepan. Gradually add cornmeal to milk, stirring constantly to prevent lumps. Cook and stir over medium heat until mixture thickens and becomes smooth. Beat egg yolks until thick and lemon colored. Blend cornmeal mixture into egg yolks. Add butter, sugar, and salt, and mix thoroughly. Using clean beater, beat egg whites until stiff, but not dry, peaks are formed. Spread egg yolk mixture over egg whites and gently fold together. Turn into greased 2 quart casserole. Bake 35 to 40 minutes or until a wooden pick comes out clean when inserted in center. Serve immediately out of the oven, topped with lots of butter. Serves 6 to 8.

CYBILL SHEPHERD

The cool, blue-eyed blonde from Tennessee got her start when she became Memphis Miss Teenage, which eventually led her to the East Coast and a successful modeling career in New York City. In 1971, she made a sensational film debut as the small-town temptress in *The Last Picture Show,* and then went on to star in several other films. Following a performance in television's *The Yellow Rose,* she settled firmly into place as the funny, popular Maddy Hayes, owner of a detective agency in the television series, *Moonlighting.*

"This corn bread should be served immediately out of the oven. Spoon it onto the plate, top with lots of butter — and be sure to eat with a spoon."

61

PERFECT TEN BROWNIES

4 squares unsweetened chocolate

⅓ cup butter

2 eggs

½ cup sugar

½ cup sifted all purpose flour

1 teaspoon vanilla extract

½ cup granola

Preheat oven to 350°. Grease 8″ × 8″ pan. Melt chocolate and butter together. In a bowl, beat eggs with sugar until fluffy. Add chocolate mixture and blend. Add flour and vanilla and stir until mixed. Spread mixture in pan and garnish with granola. Bake 25 minutes. Cool and cut into squares. Makes approximately 12 brownies.

MARY LOU RETTON

This bouncy, pint size gymnast in the stars and stripes uniform vaulted to fame with her perfect ten score in the 1984 Olympics. Her dad was a former West Virginia basketball player and rookie with the Yankees, so she comes by it honestly. She has a string of firsts to her credit, including first female to be inducted into the Olympics Hall of Fame and first female to grace a Wheaties box. A true champion, she continues her rigorous training at Bela Karolyi's school in Houston.

"Brownies are my favorite dessert. I cut down on the sugar and add granola for more energy to keep me going."

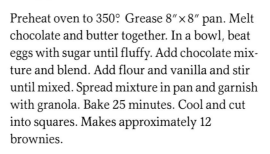

The Southwest

CARL SONTHEIMER
ANNE GREER

The cuisine of the Southwest, or Tex-Mex as it is fondly nicknamed, has been enriched by several cultures but it originated with those native Americans who lived in the region. To the great American agricultural triad of indigenous foods — corn, beans, and squash — were added contributions from the Mexican Indians and the Spanish. From the Aztecs came tomatoes and chilies — an offering by Emperor Montezuma II to the Spanish Conquistadores in 1519. From the Spanish, garlic and onions and a skilled and free hand with seasonings. From northwestern Mexico came the tortilla, the versatile, unleavened bread that doubles as a plate.

That Southwestern cooking is a trend as hot as four alarm chili is attested to by the number and variety of Tex-Mex recipes contributed to this book. From Erma Bombeck's Ranchero Dip to Malcolm Forbes' Trinchera Tacos, from Nancy Lopez' Enchilada Casserole to Polly Bergen's Chili for a Crowd, Tex-Mex has broken its geographic boundaries and is celebrated from sea to shining sea.

Engineer, physicist, wit, and resident genius of the Cuisinarts Company, he holds patents on a number of advanced inventions. By taking a little French machine called the Magimix, improving on it, and creating the celebrated Cuisinart food processor, he turned his avocation, cooking, into his vocation and revolutionized cooking in America. He is publisher of *The Pleasures of Cooking* magazine. Anne is an author, food columnist, and cooking teacher who has explored for almost 20 years the cooking of the Southwest. In the course of her research there, she has visited the farms, houses, and marketplaces of nearly every large Mexican-American community. Her magnus opus is *The Cooking of the Southwest* which was published by Carl Sontheimer.

"Both of us are delighted with the rapidly growing recognition of this truly American ethnic cuisine — one of the richest, most varied, and versatile in the world. It's repertory is as great as that of French cuisine — from the simplest appetizer such as the skewered grilled meats, called anticuchos, to the wide variety of classic dessert flans."

CHOCOLATE MOUNTAIN PEAKS

Crumb Crust

1 pound chocolate chip cookies

2 tablespoons butter

Preheat oven to 350°. Process cookies and butter in food processor until mixture is completely broken down into moist crumbs. Distribute evenly around bottom of 9" spring form pan. Press crumbs firmly and evenly against bottom and up along sides of pan. Bake 12 to 15 minutes. Remove from oven and set aside.

Bottom Stratum

4 ounces (about ⅔ cup) milk chocolate chips

4 ounces (about ⅔ cup) semisweet chocolate chips

½ cup (1 stick) butter

½ cup heavy cream (divided)

6 egg yolks

In heavy metal sauce pan over low heat, melt butter and chocolate together, stirring constantly. Add half of the cream and continue stirring until cream is fully blended into chocolate. Add egg yolks, one at a time, stirring each until fully incorporated into chocolate mixture. Continue to stir for 3 minutes; add remainder of cream and stir until fully blended. Remove from heat and pour into crumb shell. Place in refrigerator to cool.

Middle Stratum

6 ounces (½ cup) semisweet chocolate chips

1¼ cups heavy cream (divided)

3 tablespoons confectioners' sugar

In saucepan, over medium heat, melt chocolate in ¾ cup of the cream, stirring until fully blended. Place saucepan in bowl of ice (or place briefly in freezer) until mixture is cooled. In chilled mixing bowl, combine sugar with remaining very cold cream. Turn mixer on low and add chocolate/cream mixture to sugar/cream mixture. After mixture is fully blended, increase mixer speed to medium and continue mixing until mixture holds soft peaks when beaters are pulled away. Remove pie from refrigerator and pour second filling over first filling. Spread evenly and return to refrigerator.

Top Stratum

6 ounces (1 cup) milk chocolate chips

1½ cups heavy cream (divided)

3 tablespoons confectioners' sugar

Follow instructions for Middle Stratum. Remove pie from refrigerator and pour third filling over second filling. Spread evenly and then use spatula and "a twist of the wrist" to form deep valleys and peaks in the Chocolate Mountain Peaks of goodness. Return to refrigerator. Chill at least 1 hour before serving. Peaks may be dusted with confectioners' sugar "snow" just before serving. Serves 10.

Shopping information: the 3 chocolate fillings, in addition to other ingredients, require a total of 10 ounces milk chocolate chips, 10 ounces semisweet chocolate chips, and 3¼ cups heavy cream.

MRS. FIELDS

One of four good looking, good cooking sisters, she specialized in Toll House cookies in the family kitchen. She parlayed her expertise into a multimillion dollar enterprise headquartered in the ski resort town of Park City, Utah. Following her strict rule that the cookies are sold warm from the oven, she donates all cooled-down cookies to local charities.

"This mountain of chocolate goodness was inspired by the beautiful peaks of the Wasatch Mountain Range."

INSTANT COFFEE

Add one heaping teaspoonful of instant coffee, any good brand, to a cup of boiling hot water. Allow to cool slightly and drink slowly. Repeat as necessary.

"I have often told of my favorite recipe. It combines excellent flavor with economy of effort."

Editor's note: This recipe can be usefully employed in Cheryl Ladd's Raw Apple Cake, page 60, or in that grande finale to any meal, Café Brûlot, the recipe for which follows:

Café Brûlot

Peel of 1 lemon, cut in a long spiral

Peel of 1 orange, cut in a long spiral

6 cloves

2 cups prepared instant coffee, black and hot

2 cinnamon sticks

10 sugar cubes

1½ ounces orange flavored brandy

1½ ounces cognac

6 strips lemon peel

Stud each lemon and orange spiral with 3 cloves. Pierce and securely intertwine the peels on a fork. Pour coffee into flameproof bowl and add cinnamon sticks. Place 5 sugar cubes in large ladle. Pour orange flavored brandy into ladle, ignite, and pour over fork-entwined peels into coffee. Repeat procedure with remaining sugar cubes and the cognac. Place forked peels in coffee; let stand 1 minute and remove. Pour 3 ounces Café Brûlot into a demitasse. Twist lemon strip above drink and drop into cup. Repeat. Yield: 6 servings.

JOHN KENNETH GALBRAITH

Writer, economist, and political pundit, he has the gift of making economics comprehensible to the layman. His book *The Affluent Society* was a best seller. Called into government service by John F. Kennedy, who appointed him ambassador to India, he later became a speechwriter for President Johnson. He was, until his retirement in 1975, the James M. Warburg Professor of Economics at Harvard. Married with three sons, he resides in Marlboro, Vermont.

1791

Chocolate
Finale

Every celebrated chef knows that the quickest way to
a culinary reputation is through a repertoire of sensational
chocolate desserts. Guaranteed to delight the most
discerning guests are these specialties by John Glenn, John and
Anjelica Huston, Robert Motherwell, and Mary Lou Retton.

VIRGINIA ★★★★★★★

HARD-SHELL CRABS IN BEER©

6 dozen live hard-shell crabs
3 cans beer
Tabasco sauce
Salt and pepper

Pour beer in a big pot. Add Tabasco, a bit of salt and pepper, and toss in crabs only when the beer is boiling hot. Put on a pot lid slightly smaller than the kettle and weight it down good to hold the crabs down. Let them steam until they turn red—about 15 minutes. Forget the tablecloth, forget the plates. Spread out newspapers and plenty of paper napkins and as many nutcrackers as you can dig up. Serve with melted butter for dipping and crusty bread for mopping up the juice. Serves 6 to 8.

Editor's note: Additional accompaniments traditionally served with hard-shell crabs are lemon juice, tartar sauce, celery stalks, green olives, Tabasco sauce, dill pickles, and oyster crackers. Dessert is watermelon served on freshly spread newspapers.

© 1973 by Pearl Bailey by permission of Harcourt, Brace, Jovanovich, Inc.

PEARL BAILEY

Her attitude towards life—that it is so full and rich—and her extremely human quality have endeared Pearlie Mae to the nation. Born in Newport News, Virginia, she got her show business start at the age of 13 by following her famous brother, tapdancer Bill Bailey, on the Washington, D.C. small club circuit, then sang with Count Basie and his orchestra. Although she starred in such Broadway hits as *St. Louis Woman,* this preacher's daughter is best known for her soulful recordings of songs like *Takes Two to Tango,* and *Legalize My Name.* At 60, she enrolled as a freshman at Georgetown University and now holds a B.A. in Theology. This recipe is adapted from her remarkable cookbook, *Pearl's Kitchen,* which is infused with her incomparable colloquialisms and "down home" wisdom.

"I'm delighted you decided to use my Hard-Shell Crabs in Beer recipe 'cause it's really a delicious dish—smiles."

1788

The South

The hospitality of the South may be best recalled by the variety and splendor of its cooking which is expressed in a variety of local styles each using an abundance of fresh produce. In Florida alone, there are 6,972,000 acres of citrus groves yielding 570,800 tons of fruit. And while the Sunshine State has given its name to oranges, the Carolinas have given their name to rice, the Gulf to shrimp, and Virginia to ham.

Begin the gourmet trail along salt-sprayed Cheasapeake Bay, wend across plantation country to Blue Grass farms, follow along the Blue Ridge Mountains through the Carolinas, touch on the Swamps, linger in Cajun and Creole country, and end up in the Keys. And anywhere and everywhere along the way there's good regional cooking, good cooks to create it, and good company to share it with.

DINAH SHORE

Singer, writer, athlete, and cook, she started to enjoy enormous popularity during her three year run on Eddie Cantor's weekly radio program on NBC in the 1950s. Her popularity grew with her Sunday night television series *The Dinah Shore Show,* which won five Emmys. Today she is a household name and one of the Gallop Poll's 10 most admired women. Born Frances Rose Shore in Winchester, Tennessee, she had her own radio show in Nashville before teaming up in New York with another young singer, Frank Sinatra. She landed her first New York job with her audition song *Dinah,* and the rest is recording history. She's an accomplished cook, too, and her first cookbook, *Someone's in the Kitchen with Dinah,* has been reprinted 21 times.

"The South is ever green groves of lemons and limes, of grapefruits and oranges. The South is peaches, pecans, and peanuts. The South is terrapin and crab, ham and fried chicken. The South is collard greens, okra, and black-eyed peas. But the South's grandest product is hospitality."

BITTERSWEET CHOCOLATE MOUSSE

3 3 ounce bars of Lindt extra bittersweet chocolate with vanilla, or any good quality bittersweet chocolate

5 tablespoons cold water

6 large eggs, separated

2 teaspoons dark rum (optional)

Break chocolate into small pieces and put in heavy iron or enamel pan. Add water and stir constantly with wooden spoon over very low heat until chocolate melts. Remove pan from heat and cool slightly. (Chocolate mixture should be warm, not hot, or eggs will curdle.) Carefully stir egg yolks into chocolate with spoon. Stir briskly until well blended. Beat in rum, if desired. Beat egg whites until very stiff. Transfer chocolate mixture to large bowl. With spoon or whisk, carefully fold egg whites into chocolate. Pour into large glass bowl or eight individual bowls. Refrigerate for 6 hours before serving. Serves 8.

ROBERT MOTHERWELL

Considered the most articulate of the abstract expressionists, this early member of the New York School helped to forge the postwar art movement that gained America recognition as a cultural power. Although born in Aberdeen, Washington, he draws inspiration for his oil and watercolor paintings such as *Spanish Elegy* and *The Voyage* from the modern European masters, French romantic literature, and current events. He is a renaissance man, and his fine taste extends to food, to be sure, as evidenced by this delectable dish.

"This is a rich mousse that may not be sweet enough for some dessert lovers. It's good served with a half pint of heavy cream which has been whipped with four tablespoons of sugar and a dash of vanilla or rum. The beauty of this elegant dish is that it can be prepared in under 20 minutes."

1889

APPLE PIE

Pastry

½ cup butter

½ cup margarine

2 cups flour

3 to 4 tablespoons ice water

Cut butter and margarine into flour with knife or pastry blender until consistency of corn-meal. Add ice water gradually, working in just enough to hold ingredients together. Roll into rectangle on lightly floured board to 1" thickness. Refrigerate for 20 minutes. Roll out again, this time to a thickness of ⅛". Line shallow baking pan (15" × 10") with this prepared pastry.

11 to 12 medium apples

1 cup sugar

1 tablespoon cinnamon

Juice of ½ lemon

½ cup maple syrup

Sharp cheddar cheese, sliced

Preheat oven to 450°. Peel, core, and cut each apple into 6 sections. Arrange in one layer on the pastry in pan. Mix sugar and cinnamon and sprinkle over the apples. Sprinkle lemon juice on top. Bake 20 minutes. Reduce heat to 350° and bake another 25 minutes. Drizzle maple syrup over top and serve warm with a slice of cheese. Serves 10.

JAY AND SHARON ROCKEFELLER

Carrying on the Rockefeller tradition of public service, this great grandson of the oil billionaire was a two term Governor of West Virginia before being elected a U.S. Senator from his adopted state. He is married to Sharon Percy, board member of the Corporation for Public Broadcasting and daughter of former Illinois Senator Charles Percy. The Rockefellers have four children, born and raised in the Mountain State.

"This family recipe is a great American dessert that generations of Rockefellers enjoy."

1863

71

LIPTAUER CHEESE

5 8 ounce packages cream cheese

3 tablespoons capers

2 tablespoons onions, finely chopped

1 tube anchovy paste

2 teaspoons dry mustard

2 teaspoons paprika

4 tablespoons chopped chives

1 tablespoon caraway seed

Beer

Mix all together until well blended. Soften with beer to make the right consistency for spreading, being careful not to make it too thin. Serve with potato chips or crackers. Makes 5 cups.

PECAN PIE

½ cup butter

⅔ cup sugar

3 eggs

½ teaspoon salt

1 cup light corn syrup

½ cup medium cream

1 teaspoon vanilla extract

1 cup pecans, coarsely chopped

9" unbaked pastry shell

Whole pecan halves

Sweetened whipped cream

Preheat oven to 350°. Cream together butter and sugar. When very light, add eggs, one at a time. Beat well. Add salt, corn syrup, cream, vanilla, and chopped pecans. Mix thoroughly. Pour into pastry shell. Bake 40 minutes or until firm. About 10 minutes before end of baking time, decorate with pecan halves. Serve with sweetened whipped cream.

SHARON GLESS AND TYNE DALY

Two of "New York's Finest" in the hit television series, *Cagney and Lacey,* grace the Badger State page by virtue of Tyne Daly's (Lacey) birth in Madison, Wisconsin. Sharon Gless (Cagney) is a fifth generation Californian. So devoted is their viewing audience that fans refused to accept the program's cancellation and staged an intense phone and letter protest until the program was reinstated. Both actresses have impressive credits in regional theatre, feature films, made for television films, and serials. Off camera, Sharon Gless relaxes by reading, playing poker, and collecting cookbooks. Tyne Daly and her director husband George Stanford Brown recently had their third child. Not since *I Love Lucy* has a serial baby been so anticipated.

About the Liptauer cheese recipe, Sharon says, "This is one of my favorites—it's from my grandmother's cookbook, written in 1947." About her pecan pie recipe, Tyne says eloquently, "Yumm!"

1848

RIVERBANK TROUT

1 strip bacon, per person
1 trout, per person
Seasoned salt
Lemon juice
Onion slices
Butter
Lemons, thinly sliced
Limes, thinly sliced

Cook bacon lightly, reserving drippings. Rub outside and cavity of trout with bacon drippings and seasoned salt. Sprinkle cavity generously with lemon juice, then fill with bacon strip, onion slices, and dabs of butter. Place trout on piece of foil large enough to enclose completely. Arrange lemon and lime slices on top of trout. Wrap tightly in foil. Cook 5 minutes on each side over hot charcoal. Do not overcook.

CURT GOWDY

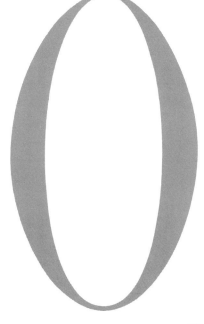

Ever since his first coast to coast broadcast in 1949, his Wyoming twang and colorful style have enlivened broadcasts of the Olympics, World Series, and numerous big bowl games. He has been named Sportscaster of the Year, has received the George Foster Peabody Award, and has been named to the Baseball Hall of Fame. He is also one of the best sports fishermen in the world.

"This dish is a great enjoyment on any trout stream in America. We always stop in the middle of the day on our float trips. We have a salad prepared in advance, baked beans and potatoes, and the tastes are great — especially when cooked in the great outdoors."

INDEX ★★★★★★